W9-AEN-914

Religion
and the Modern World

UNIVERSITY OF PENNSYLVANIA
BICENTENNIAL CONFERENCE

Religion
and the Modern World

By

JACQUES MARITAIN
JOSEPH L. HROMÁDKA
WILLIAM J. McGARRY
JOHN A. RYAN
PAUL J. TILLICH
ROBERT L. CALHOUN
CHARLES W. GILKEY
REINHOLD NIEBUHR
RUFUS M. JONES
ROBERT E. L. STRIDER
JOHN A. MACKAY
HENRY ST. GEORGE TUCKER
MORRIS S. LAZARON
HENRY NOBLE MacCRACKEN
GEORGE NAUMAN SHUSTER

57587

BR41
P4
1941

UNIVERSITY OF PENNSYLVANIA PRESS
Philadelphia
1941

BR41.P4 1941 ST. JOSEPH'S UNIVERSITY STX
Religion and the modern world,

3 9353 00151 4916

Copyright 1941

UNIVERSITY OF PENNSYLVANIA PRESS

Manufactured in the United States of America
by The Haddon Craftsmen, Inc., Camden, N. J.

BX 51
M 34 r

Contents

Contemporary Renewals in Religious Thought

By

JACQUES MARITAIN, D. EN PH.*

MY ADDRESS deals with trends in religious thought. I will divide it in two parts. The first will treat of historical aspects of the question. The second will touch upon a few problems which directly concern religious thought and which seems to me especially important.

I

Let us begin with a few historical notes. We have not enough time to go into a detailed exposition; I should like merely to sketch the main lines and point out the most characteristic tendencies.

As to religious thought developing out of the Reformation, you know that after Lessing, Kant, and Schleiermacher, a process of rationalization of religion was the dominant tendency of the nineteenth century. In Germany notably, so-called liberal theology and biblical criticism of the rationalist type triumphed with the well-known Harnack. Later in England and America, in spheres not yet exegetical or theological, but merely philosophical, a remarkable movement developed, attempting to interpret and to justify religious feelings on the basis of a kind of Integral Empiricism. This was the period when Pragmatists and Pluralists tried to save the idea of God by claiming that this idea gives greater breadth to one's vision of the world, greater resonance to metaphysics, and also makes the world seem less strange and more intimate to us; for in order to be courageous in life and its undertakings we need a powerful ally with whom to exchange personal services; finally, they attempted this be-

---

* Professor de Philosophie, l'Institut Catholique de Paris et l'Institut d'Etudes Medievales de Toronto, Visiting Professor at Columbia and Princeton Universities.

cause the world of religious experience has its place amidst the multiple Pluralistic universes, and because the religious experiences of everyone are so many revelations of the super-human.

But is this God really God? one may ask. William James assures us that God is synonymous with *that which is ideal in things*. Borrowing certain suggestions of John Stuart Mill in his *Essays on Religion*, the Pluralists said that God exists in time, for only abstractions exist outside of time; they said that He is not infinite and could not be perfect because, as Professor Mac-Taggart explained, His perfection would destroy the equilibrium of the universal Commonwealth. He is not omniscient, added William James; since He is not a finite personality, God cannot know everything. The vastest subject that exists can, however, lack knowledge of many other subjects, he said. Who knows, perhaps God lacks some knowledge of Pluralism.

God is not all-powerful since divine almightiness would be incompatible with the absolute individuality of persons. It was consistent with such premises for William James to grant some likeliness to polytheism—a republican-minded hypothesis which the French philosopher Renouvier had held for a time. In any event it was agreeable to Pluralist tendencies to hold that perhaps without our aid God would be overcome in the struggle. Finally, it is we who help Him exist. We must be companions of the sorrow of God said Scotus Novanticus (M. Laurie). Such a formula, as true and profound in the case of the incarnate God, as it is vain in the case of God in his divine nature, shows how the dogma of the Incarnation amongst those who no longer believe it reacts by some singular compensation upon the notion itself of the divine essence.

Briefly speaking, as a French critic* wrote, "The God of Pragmatists was an old faithful servant designed to help us carry our cross and drag our burden in the midst of sweat and dust and daily trials." This is the God that makes the books of Mr. Wells a success. "God is not absolute, God is finite," promulgated the author of *The Time Machine*. "A finite God who battles in his grandiose and large manner, as we battle in our manner, weakly and without knowing how to go about it, who is with us, who is our ally, this is the essence of any real religion."

* Bourdeau, *Pragmatisme et Modernisme*.

The assertions just cited are the normal result of a method which is not concerned with the truth. You forbid yourselves reasonable speech once you begin by rejecting logic and refusing the use of the steeled, spiritual, discerning instrument of intelligence, precisely there where the object of knowledge is of a pure immaterial nature and defies every effort of the imagination and the senses.

The philosophers of old, aware of the sublimity of such an object, equipped their minds, to approach it, with the resources of the highest science; they trained their minds in the art of making distinctions; they anointed it with the various perfumes of contemplation and meditation, and they dared to *stammer about divine things* only after a long struggle for intellectual purification. Having worked out over a period of centuries the accurate instrument of analogical knowledge, they succeeded thus, as in the case of Thomas Aquinas, in showing how to reconcile rationally all the oppositions which first stump reason, and which must necessarily do so, inasmuch as reason thinking about God speculates with the measure of the sensible world. For these oppositions are nothing but the evidence itself of the infinite transcendence of the deity. Indeed, the Divine mode of these conciliations escaped their analysis—for here the reality to be grasped overflows all our concepts—and from this viewpoint metaphysics opened out upon mystery, as every science does, moreover, to a certain degree. But at least it was known with perfect certitude that not the slightest interruption had occurred in the thread of logical necessities, and that there was nothing in this mystery contrary to reason, so that metaphysics could assume to itself the striking phrase of St. Lawrence: "My night has no darkness."

The philosophers of Absolute Empiricism had adopted an opposite course. The more difficult and profound a problem was, the more they decided to utilize sensory appearances interpreted according to the mere postulates of ethical practice, and to be satisfied with the most rough and ready and easy solutions provided these had a counterpart in action. Despite all the touching and even validly directed contents of the infrarational feelings they depended upon, it was inevitable that their God be nothing more than some God of the flies, the phantom god of moral Phenomenism.

The currents of religious thought arising from Pragmatism and Pluralism have been largely outgrown today both in the Old and the New World. I emphasized them briefly because they show us that if we hope to see an authentic religious renaissance, we must abandon once and for all the bias of Empiricism and we must also understand that to meet successfully Hegelian Monism, it is necessary to begin by not remaining half-Hegelian, and by uprooting from our thought the primary error of Hegel, which was that of placing reason and philosophy above faith and religion—emptied by this very fact of their own substance.

In truth, in the background of all more or less non-dogmatic religious thought of the nineteenth century stands the great figure of Hegel, who must ever be borne in mind. Some followed one or another of the numberless currents flowing from his philosophy; others, on the contrary, tried to go against these currents; he was present everywhere; all underwent his influence in some way or other. This is particularly true of those who, reacting against Bradley, and shaking the temple or the prison of Monism, as Samsons breaking their chains, continued nevertheless to work in the shadow of Hegel.

All the tendencies mentioned so far were directed towards a humanization of religion. The age was optimistic; it held that man all by himself, using either reason or experience, was marching towards the Jerusalem of light, and that his science, his critical and historical method, and his philosophy were the supreme rules of interpretation to which the contents of Revelation were subjected, in so far as the word Revelation still had some meaning. God was God, and merited our reverence because we could justify Him, and because He vouchsafed superior security to the progress of our nature. These notions seemed final; as sure as our civilization itself. In a curious encounter, moreover, the Naturalism and the Humanism of the period resulted in dissolving nature in a process of dissociation ad infinitum due to an entirely ideal analysis, and in dissolving the human person in the impersonality of facts and relations between facts to which the Positivist viewpoint reduced reality. The reaction of Pragmatism and Pluralism was from this viewpoint validly oriented; but, as I tried to point out above, it was doomed to ineffectuality.

Long before visible historic events brought cruel disillusionment to the naturalist optimism of the nineteenth century, the spiritual experience and mysterious destiny of a recluse full of anguish and prophetic instinct opened the road in the Protestant world to entirely different movements of thought; Kierkegaard played in these movements of thought a capital rôle, whose importance cannot be exaggerated. This time Hegel in person is attacked; Kierkegaard's drama consisted of rediscovering the absolute of faith by turning against, even if it bruised him most cruelly, the whole universe of Hegelianism, in the midst of which, however, his mind continued to breathe; he turned against the very root of this universe, against the idea that the supreme moment of dialectic and the supreme judgment of things of the spirit belong to philosophy and not to religion. Kierkegaard appeared under many guises because he lived in the midst of contradiction and because the burning intuition within him, that he wanted to manifest to men, on all sides met with impossibilities—the impossibilities that Hegelian reason built around him. This intuition could not be conceptualized into a doctrine, it reverberated into symbolic attempts and contrasting figures. With his brilliant and many-sided intelligence, Kierkegaard was neither professional philosopher nor Theologian. He was a restless and suffering man, attracted by the world and tormented by the longing for holiness, and singularly rich in mystical gifts and insights. Certain pages written by him on the spiritual darkness of the soul seeking God reveal with an unmistakable accent profound mystical experience. Truly speaking there is for Kierkegaard only one problem, the problem of faith; but it was postulated for him in tragic terms. For on the one hand, it is by denying the world of reason and logic, the value of which he knew so well, however, but incarnate to his mind in Hegel, that he was able to affirm the reality of faith. On the other hand, Kierkegaard's faith, lacking, by reason of a defective idea of the Church, the adherence to a body of doctrine publicly revealed, was itself a skinned faith, stripped of every element of certitude and security—and consequently the more linked to anguish and interior laceration as it was real in the substance of his soul. His personal experience here played a decisive rôle. Having decided for reasons of conscience to break off his engagement to a girl whom he loved and who loved him, he looked upon this sacrifice after the type of Abraham's sacrifice, and he believed that if he truly had the faith of Abraham a miracle would occur, and his fiancée would be returned to him as Isaac was to his father. But his fiancée was never given back to him. His profound sense of the impenetrable mystery of faith within us, and the disproportion between divine things and the entire collection of what is visible and of human significances, even within consciousness, led him, under the impulse of this experience, as under the influence of his irrationalism, to think that the man of faith necessarily lives in a crucifying doubt in regard to faith itself—it would be a blasphemy of faith to believe that one has it—and led him to condemn as an idol of human security all that is solidly established, assured, and enjoyed even in divine certitudes. In this state of laceration, in this rending of man, there reappeared simultaneously, with unbearable effulgence, the world of miracles, the world of Divine Liberty, the pure and naked affirmation of the exigencies of God, the ineffable and terrifying relation of person to person between God and man, all that the Naturalism and the Humanism of the nineteenth century sought to efface.

The influence of Kierkegaard was decisive in the new religious movements that developed in the Nordic and German worlds before the coming of Nazism to power; the most prominent representative of these new movements is the theologian Karl Barth. The doctrines of Harnack and liberal exegesis are completely discarded. Barth undertakes to go back to the reformers, to the primitive data of Lutheranism and especially Calvinism, not without, however, contributing to scriptural exegesis, and to theology henceforth linked to dialectics rather than to history, the effort of an extremely vigilant mind, well informed on the problems of our times. From the very beginning, Barthian theology appears as a very definite counter-Humanism. Nothing is valuable but the Word of God received in the integrity of its unfathomable affirmations, and scrutinized with ardent obedience, not by human reason which is worthless, but by faith. By one of those strange encounters, to which the ebb and flow of human history have accustomed us, Barthian Protestantism, while actually rediscovering many Catholic positions, reproaches Catholicism for the very opposite things for which liberal Protestantism reproached it; it is no longer reproached for believing in unchangeable revealed data, in the supernatural, in the fact of miracles, but for not immolating everything else to them; no longer for being hostile to nature and reason, as was claimed so long, but for honoring nature and reason too much. On these, as on the very principle of the Reformation, on the relations of nature and of grace, on the exact meaning of the mystery of justification, on the rôle of charity, on the structure and authority of the mystical body of Christ, the opposition between Barth and us remains irreducible, though admitting exchange of views and mutual respect.

For Karl Barth, when God enters into man, He comes like a powerful armed conqueror, like an irresistible enemy, shrouded in his incomprehensibility as in thunder; and dispersing all weapons of man and of human reason in order to strip the vanquished of them. It is not surprising then that Barth makes a diabolus in theologia of that kind of knowledge that Thomists call analogy of proper proportionality and which is in their eyes the royal road to know God, either naturally from created things, or supernaturally through the super-analogy of faith, through the mysterious analogies that God Himself uses to declare Himself to us. Barth is an enemy of philosophy, natural ethics, natural theology. It is, however, noteworthy that in this drama and conflict between God and man, wherein faith subdues our rebellious nature, the vanquished becomes conscious of himself and of his personality much more profoundly than does the man of paganism, because, as I said in connection with Kierkegaard, it is between the Divine personality and the human person that the play is finally played, with all the directness, ineffability, imprevision, and peril that are involved in relationships and conflicts of person to person. In a somewhat tragic setting—truly a hopelessly illogical one, because it destroys in the order of nature what is affirmed in the order of grace—the human person emerges by virtue of Christ from the débris of a sacked nature. On the other hand, deeper reflection led Barth to try, by means of especially subtle dialectic, to restore—defectively indeed—all the human and cultural values he could restore within a system of thought which originally, and of itself, tends to deny these values and the order of earthly culture.

May I add that like Kierkegaard, although in an entirely different manner, Karl Barth has to face in the depth of himself a sort of substantial antinomy. For him all in the world is worthless except the Word of God heard in the inner recesses of the heart. Still he is a theologian and must himself speak. He would seem to be anxiously questioning himself and continually wondering whether this ardent word which is so stimulating to his followers and has renewed Protestant theology, is the word of Karl Barth or the Word of God.

The tendencies mentioned up to now have developed within Protestant thought. Among the orthodox, most recent developments began in Russia before the October Revolution and continue since in exile; the most outstanding figure is Nicholas Berdiaeff, whose work is highly significant for the present epoch. With Berdiaeff, also, the mystery of faith—but this time a faith operating in reason—occupies a central position. Berdiaeff is not a theologian like Karl Barth; he is a philosopher, and all his thinking is situated on the plane of Christian philosophy—a Christian philosophy rather differently conceived from ours, moreover. And he is a prophetic philosopher, or rather, for him philosophy, inspired by faith, finds its normal term in a prophetic function. Well acquainted with Jacob Boehme, Schelling, and Franz von Baader, on the one hand, and on the other with Catholic spiritual writers, he pursues his speculations in the direction of an existential philosophy, as it is called today, a philosophy especially interested in the problem of spirit and freedom. I am aware that his statements on Thomism are often unjust, and I do not think that he and I can ever agree on the first principles of metaphysics. But even while arguing with him, one always gets from him that precious stimulus which comes from the absolute sincerity of a mind in search for being. And in the order of moral and social philosophy, and particularly the philosophy of history, or as he calls it, historiosophy, which is his favorite field of study, he provides us, along with an ethical system rich in profound moral experience and encumbered with an irritating irrationalism, fruitful concrete intuitions which clarify many of the most urgent practical problems of our times. He is one of those who still think in their hearts; he is one of the witnesses of Christian freedom.

Coming to Catholic thought, I should like to point out two

especially characteristic tendencies; first, the current of Scheler-ian thought which developed mostly in Germany; secondly, the current of Thomism which first appeared in the Roman universities and later in many countries of the Old and New Worlds, and above all in France and Belgium. There are many other currents, particularly philosophical currents, in the Catholic world; but we must confine ourselves here to those which seem most significant. I should like, however, to pay tribute first of all to a few men to whom we owe a debt of gratitude and particular admiration; to that great pauper Leon Bloy, that writer of genius who died in the last few days of the first World War. He was a prophet, too, and this in the light of the gift of tears and genuine contemplation. He spent his life denouncing the luke-warmness and the prevarications of the modern world; his burning and mighty faith affirmed in season and out of season with scandalous contempt for the powerful figures of his day; his terrible charity, his irrepressible freedom of mind, his sense of supernatural realities, and his prophetic penetration brought many souls to the path of God and greatly influenced the religious revival amongst the French intelligentsia that occurred between the two wars. I want to pay tribute also to Charles Péguy, whose spirit is alive in the best of French youth and who inspired it with the sense of the temporal vocation of the Christian; to G. K. Chesterton, whose paradoxical and savory wisdom was a knighthood of God; to Peter Wust, the kindly Augustinian philosopher who died a few months ago after a very cruel illness, and who by offering piously to God his frightful sufferings showed his friends that even there where the worst barbarism is raging, Christianity still numbers men worthy of the name; to Henry Bergson, finally, the master of my youth, who is now eighty years old, and who does not profess Catholicism yet whose influence has been great in the currents of Catholic thought. He loses no opportunity to affirm his love of Christianity, and his latest works, wherein religious experience brought him beyond a still deficient metaphysics, reveal the admirable bonds that can be established between philosophy and the testimony of Christian mystics, in whom alone he sees the fullness of the life of the spirit.

Max Scheler was not a theologian like Karl Barth nor a prophetic philosopher like Berdiaeff. He was a too philosophical philosopher, so to speak, at least in the German sense of

the word; for a quenchless thirst spurred him on ceaselessly
to reversals of viewpoint, and to new syntheses, the last of
which one was never sure would not be replaced by another.
He applied with singular perspicacity the phenomenological
method to the spiritual and moral content of human existence,
and he thus reopened within philosophy itself religious springs.
Classic analysis, with its process of artificial conceptual dissociation, gave way to a more penetrating analysis which, thanks
to its metaphysical mode, went further into psychology than
psychology itself, and which respected and brought to light the
integrity given to intuition. Thus during what was in my
opinion the happiest period of his work, Scheler was able to
lay bare to philosophy "what is eternal in man" and the
concrete implications of the superhuman gifts in the substance
of human life. Christian virtues, humility and charity, were
rehabilitated, not from a dogmatic or theological viewpoint,
but from the viewpoint of a sort of secular knowledge of the
concrete. And simultaneously, by an entirely different method
from those of Kierkegaard and Barth, and in a much more
humanist setting, he restored the meaning of person, a universe in itself. If the absence of a sufficiently firm metaphysics
and theology had not given his thought too much versatility,
if interior crises which darkened his faith, and the exterior
moral and political devastations which already began to ravage
the conscience of his country, had not prevented the work and
personal action of Max Scheler from fulfilling its promise, he
might have revived the religious life of Germany in the direction of a Christianity full of philosophical intelligence and internal life.

The historical importance of the Thomist renaissance comes
from the fact that it constitutes a vast movement of thought
affecting the life itself of the Church and the efforts of lay Christian workers, and from the fact that it consists of something
rare in intellectual work, namely, a durable and progressive
collaboration founded upon common principles and a living
tradition. Pope Leo XIII was the instigator; Cardinal Mercier
was one of the first great proponents. Theologians like Zig-
liara, del Prado, Gardeil, Garrigou-Lagrange, Charles Journet,
share in this revival as did also philosophers and poets; the
Thomist revival has also awakened the active interest of many

non-Catholic circles and many university centers, notably in England and America.

You know that in this country a metaphysical rebirth which seems very important for the future of culture is occurring under the influence of St. Thomas Aquinas, thanks especially to the work of Dr. Phelan and of Etienne Gilson at the Institute of Medieval Studies in Toronto, to the work of Mortimer Adler, and to that of many young philosophers too numerous to mention.

The tendencies that the Thomist revival represent are at once philosophical and theological. Accordingly, as Dom Chapman remarked with penetration, if one wishes to compare Thomism with modern thought, which has assumed all the divine and human problems of our destiny, one must compare modern philosophy not merely with Thomist philosophy, which is strictly limited to problems accessible to reason, but with the ensemble of Thomist philosophy and Thomist theology.

Thomism states as an absolute principle the unconditional affirmation of faith in the divine order, and it also affirms in the human order the unshakable intrinsic value of nature and reason, for every creature of God is good, as St. Paul said. Thomist thought appears from the very first as an effort to distinguish and to unite or rather to distinguish in order to unite.

Thomism can be characterized as an integralist and progressive Christian position. If we seek our conceptual weapons in the arsenal of Aristotle and Thomas Aquinas, it is not in order to return to ancient Greece or to the Middle Ages. We think that it is a sort of blasphemy against the Providence of God in history to want to go back to a past age, and we hold that there is an organic increase both in the Church and in the world. Hence the task of the Christian is, we believe, to save those "truths gone mad," as Chesterton said, which four centuries of Anthropocentric Humanism have disfigured, and to reconcile them with the truths of higher origin misunderstood by this Humanism, and to return them to Him who is Truth and to whose voice faith listens.

The Humanism of Thomas Aquinas is an Integral Humanism; I mean a Humanism which neglects nothing present in man. Such Humanism knows that man is made of nothing and that everything that comes from nothing tends of itself towards nothing; and it also knows that man is the image of God and that within man there is more than man; it knows that man is inhabited by a God who not only gives him life and activity but who gives him His Very Self and wishes him to have as final fruition the three Divine Persons.

It is a Humanism of the redemptive Incarnation—a Gospel-minded Humanism. I think that St. Thomas Aquinas is the apostle of modern times because these times have loved intelligence and have abused it and can be truly cured by it alone; and because Thomas Aquinas is the saint of the intellect; he reduces all things to the light of the Word, that Light which is at once—and this Karl Barth does not see—the Light that illuminates the reason of all men coming into this world and the Light that illuminates supernaturally all men reborn by faith. All the philosophy and all the theology of St. Thomas are constructed in the illumination of the word received by Moses: "I am Who Am."

The philosophy of St. Thomas is a philosophy not of essences but of existence; it lives from the natural intuitions of sensory experience and of the intelligence. His theology lives from faith; it is a theology of the incomprehensible Pure Act *to be* which subsists by itself and does not exist in the same way as anything exists, and whose inmost life we cannot know except by its own Word. Accordingly, it can be said that Thomist thought is above all an existential one, although it is existential in a different manner from that of the various philosophies which have adopted this term. And it must be also said that it is a personalist thought, according as the philosophic realism of St. Thomas implies at every moment the act of the entire human person, body and soul, confronted with being to penetrate; and according as the theological Transcendentalism of St. Thomas is a perpetual dialogue between Christ speaking through the Church and Scripture, and reason listening and seeking.

The synthetic character of Thomistic thought has been often emphasized, and rightly so. It tends to make for unity in man and to prepare him for that peace which surpasses all understanding, in joining or reconciling in him grace and nature, faith and reason, theology and philosophy, the supernatural virtues and the natural virtues, the spiritual order and the temporal order, the speculative order and the practical one, mystical contemplation and knowledge merely human, fidelity to eternal data and understanding of time. But this view would be incomplete if we did not add that such a reconciliation has nothing to do with the more or less easy arrangements of bookish reason; it demands repeatedly surmounting conflicts repeatedly arising; it demands of man a tension and an extension which are possible only in the agony of the Cross. For the words of St. Paul are valid also in the order of things of the spirit: "Without shedding of blood there is no redemption." The reconciliation we spoke of is a false reconciliation if it is not a redemption; and it cannot be accomplished without mysterious suffering, the focus of which is the spirit itself.

II

These considerations lead me to the points I want to discuss in the second part of this address. Two problems seem to me particularly urgent today in the domain of religious thought. The first concerns Christian philosophy and Christian politics. The second, what one might call the meaning and mission of religion itself. Naturally I shall limit myself to a few essential indications above all these.

The problem of Christian philosophy and that of Christian politics are only the speculative side and the practical side of one and the same problem. I do not think as the Barthians do that philosophy ought to disappear when confronted by faith. I do not think with the Rationalists, who are encountered not only among the disciples of Descartes and Kant and Hegel, but also among many Christians, that philosophy must accomplish its work separated from faith. I think that philosophy is the work of reason and as such is founded upon natural evidences and not upon faith, but I think that reason itself, which is not a closed world, but open, accomplishes rightly its highest works and comes to its proper fullness only when aided and vivified by the enlightenment coming from faith. The process by which philosophy has brought its autonomy into existence in regard to theology was a process normal in itself. The misfortune of modern times has been that this was accomplished under the banner of Cartesian separatism and that, instead of autonomy at a subordinate level, philosophy had claimed absolutely sovereign independence.

What the world and civilization have needed in modern times in the intellectual order, what the temporal good of men has needed for four centuries, is just Christian Philosophy.

In their place arose a separate philosophy and an inhuman Humanism, a Humanism destructive of man because it wanted to be centered upon man and not upon God. We have drained the cup, we now see before our eyes that bloody anti-Humanism, that ferocious irrationalism and trend to slavery in which rationalist Humanism finally winds up. If the world is not to sink into barbarism, a new Humanism must now come to the fore, and its task will be one of integration, of living and purifying incorporation. It will be a question of once again bringing together, vitally and organically, human reason with the irrational world of sentiment, of instinct, and emotion, as well as with the world of will and with the non-rational aspects of intellectual operations themselves. And it will be a question of once again bringing together, vitally and organically, human reason with the supra-rational and super-human world. A Humanism of this type is inconceivable if its inspiring philosophy is not a Christian philosophy, a philosophy existentially continuous with theology and faith. Many humanistic tentatives, generous in themselves, even those of Christian Humanism, such as the tentative of Erasmus and his friends, have failed because they did not start from a sufficiently high source. One type of humanism alone can reach down far enough into the recesses of the human being, and this is the Humanism which originates from the wisdom of the saints; it will take root and develop only in a regenerated civilization which will be the age of Christian-minded philosophy, an age in which science and wisdom will be reconciled under the inspiration of such a philosophy.

As to the problem of Christian politics, it has as theological presupposition what can be called the mystery of the world, the problem of the meaning of the world and the earthly commonwealth confronted with the Kingdom of God. I shall not discuss the question here, and I mention it only to point out one of the recent developments, and in my opinion a very characteristic one, in the thought of Karl Barth. It would seem that the political threat hovering over the life of souls, namely,

wars waged by the Pagan Empire against the Gospel, has stimulated him to consider more closely the function of the State
from the viewpoint of the Gospel.

In his recent writings Barth recognizes that not only Luther
but Calvin too held very defective views in this respect. His
own views also remain deficient, in my opinion, inasmuch as he
recognizes no foundation in natural law for the political order,
and holds that the State is essentially neutral, like Pontius
Pilate, in regard to the truth. Accordingly, "the State as such
knows nothing of the Spirit, of Love, of Forgiveness." However, he attempts to justify the political order and the State
from the viewpoint of the Gospel Revelation and to show that
the State when demonized, as he says, is untrue to the essence
of State, that Pilate in condemning Jesus departed from the
normal line of State, and that not only is the State bound to be
just, but also "in its substance, in its dignity, in its function
and in its relatively autonomous destination, it must serve the
purpose of Christ." Hence it follows that, faced by diverse
kinds of States, Christians are not surrounded by gray cats in
the dark, but must distinguish between this State and that,
and "would become objectively and factually enemies of the
State, if, when the power of the State threatens the freedom
of the word of God, they did not resist, or concealed the resistance which is theirs."

For Karl Barth what concerns the order of Redemption in
the political order remains largely negative and consists only in
the State's not hindering the freedom of preaching the Gospel.
In my opinion, this all too simple view still disregards the
dynamism of our wounded nature as well as of the power of
the evangelical leaven. The manner in which Christianity is to
inspire civilization must be a positive and intrinsic one, I
mean in the actual order of earthly civilization, in its profane
and temporal structures, and not merely in its relation with
the sacred order and in the support that it offers the Church.
For the political order and political virtues belong essentially
to the domain of nature, but in the existential reality of human
communities, nature itself and natural law can avoid deviations
and can attain their fullness only on the condition of being
internally vivified by those energies which originate from
Grace. The autonomy of the temporal order, like that of
philosophy, is a benefit acquired in the course of modern times.

But this autonomy can avoid leading to disaster only if, far from being a divorce, it implies an organic union with the spiritual order, an internal vivification by it. Thus it is to the ideal of a new Christendom that we must direct our hopes.

The problem of Christian politics is one of life and death for our times. The evils overwhelming the world today are exactly the final result of the idea current in the classic age according to which politics cannot and must not be Christian because it is considered a pure technique, an art intrinsically independent of ethics and religion, and whose only law is the quickest material success by any means at all, provided only they are efficacious. Truly this made a doctrine out of the perversion of politics. We think, on the contrary, that politics, no matter how extensive the part of art in it, is essentially a special branch of ethics; because it is directed towards the common good, which is an essentially human good, not merely a material good, but also and principally moral, and which supposes justice, and demands to be lasting and therefore to foment good and virtue in man. And if politics is essentially something ethical, it demands, in view of the actual state of humanity, and in order not to go astray and to reach a sufficient degree of maturity, to be helped and strengthened through everything man receives, in social existence itself, from Gospel Revelation and the Word of God operating within him. The authors of the Declaration of Independence and the Constitution of this country understood this clearly, and this makes their accomplishment so precious in the eyes of all those who believe that the Gospel is efficacious, not only for heaven but for earth. A Christian politics is neither a theocratic or clerical politics, nor a politics of pseudo-evangelical weakness and non-resistance to evil. It is a politics truly political, in other words, aware that it is situated in the order of nature and of natural virtues, and working in this order, equipped with real and concrete justice, with force, with perspicacity, with prudence, and holding the sword, the attribute of the State. It also knows that peace is the work not only of justice, but of love; it knows that men, the earthly welfare of whom is its direct aim, have an eternal destiny and are called to be adopted sons of God; accordingly, it is not neutral regarding the truth, but listens to it as far as possible, and in its own order, which is the order of nature, it knows, in the degree commensurate with its own ends, something of the Spirit, of love, and of forgiveness.

If all these considerations are true, and for my part I am convinced that they are, we must conclude that absolute Machiavellianism, such as we see it in action now in the world, must normally triumph over relative, more or less attenuated or restrained types of Machiavellianism, such as experienced in less enlightened centuries, but that absolute Machiavellianism itself, with all its victories, crowns, and conquests, is merely an immense and bloody political illusion, a kind of destroying voodoo which has no more political stability than a plague or famine; having transformed politics into an art of producing man's misfortune, it tends of itself towards a dialectic of misfortune, wherein increasingly dismal forms of misfortune endlessly follow one another.

There is another point that I should have liked to discuss today, namely, the position of the human person.

For lack of time, I will limit myself to indicating in a few words what I consider the essentials.

When the Apostles replied to the Sanhedrin, which wanted to forbid them to preach the name of Jesus: "It is better for us to obey God rather than men," they affirmed at once the freedom of the Word of God, and the transcendence of the human person called and redeemed by Him, and raised by Grace to Divine adoption; but implicitly they affirmed at the same time the transcendence of the human person in the order of nature, inasmuch as Person is a spiritual totality made for the absolute. It is one of the essential tasks of religious thought today to bring to light this natural transcendence, which is proper to the human person in the measure that it is called to achievements of a higher order than time.

I come now to the second problem, crucial, in my opinion, for religious thought in these days and which I should like to discuss briefly before terminating this address, and which concerns the meaning and mission of religion itself. Truly speaking, this problem was posited and answered by the Gospel, when the New Law succeeding the Old Testament and the theocracy of Israel, taught men the primacy of the interior over the exterior, of the spirit over the letter, of the life of Grace over external observances. But in concrete existence and

practical action, each age of civilization brings us its own
interrogation—in new forms, asking us if we know of what
manner of spirit we are, and obliging us to set working again,
if we want to remain faithful to that spirit, the word we have
heard.

Today it is especially regarding the relations between the
political and religious spheres that the interrogation is made
of us. Let me say in brief, that one of the all-important though
frequently unperceived conflicts lying at the bottom of the
sufferings of our age is the conflict which sets in opposition
among many believers two different conceptions of religion,
or rather two different ways of tending towards the realization
of religion in existence. The one is a political-minded conception, the other is a Gospel-minded conception of religion. In
regard to the spiritual ends themselves, which consist in the
good of souls and which concern the Kingdom of God, the first
conception—practically, that is, and not in the evaluation of
principles—gives *primary* importance either to the equipment
of social works and of temporal institutions, which religion
necessarily employs, or to the political means or political sup-
ports which assist it here below in its mission. The second conception does not deny the importance of this temporal equipment or of this political support; but in practice as well as in
theory it gives *primary* importance to means and forces of the
evangelical order, to the vital and hidden energies of religion
itself, to Faith operating through Charity rather than to the
Law.

The insidious and paradoxical character of this conflict
arises from the fact that it lies in the domain of practical reason
and the concrete meaning of life rather than in the domain of
speculative reason and the understanding of dogmas. As a
result, between men professing the same faith with equal sincerity a profound practical split can sometimes be observed, so
that at times political-minded believers feel less close to Gospel-
minded believers than to unbelievers who are champions of
order, even totalitarian; and sometimes Gospel-minded believers feel less close to political-minded believers than to unbelievers devoted to tolerance and freedom.

In modern times, and especially in times like ours, in which
events disconcert all efforts of human reason, the evils caused
by the political conception of religion were all the greater as

this conception is accompanied in many cases by a very defective knowledge of political realities themselves. Christian people found themselves consequently exposed to all manner of illusions. Confronted by opposite but similarly baneful and destructive forms of the anti-Christian revolution now seeking empire over the world, Christian people oftentimes deemed it necessary to choose among them instead of opposing all of them at once. An obscure process of leniency towards totalitarian forms that lying propaganda tries to picture as the upholders of order, has thus invaded a part of the believing groups in many countries. The lesson taught by events, by persecutions, by cynical agreements, and by crimes against humanity, enlightens them only little by little and leaves them in a state of mental confusion and paralysis before a drama long since begun, in which the question is whether or not men can still hope in Christianity, I do not say only to bring them to Heaven, but I say to teach them to live on earth in a way worthy of the spirit that constitutes their nobility. The seriousness of this misfortune for the world as well as for religion itself cannot be measured.

I firmly believe that the Gospel-minded conception of religion will finally prevail over the political-minded conception, and that more than ever Christians will enter into the labors and sorrows of the world but in order to carry into it the flame and life of a faith truly free from the world. I believe that the spiritual will be delivered from the various kinds of infeudation in corrupt temporal structures from which it suffers today. But if we do not want this deliverance to occur on the ruins of the world, we must fulfill it first in ourselves, and we must rediscover the meaning of that great reversal of values, of that spiritual revolution of which Christ was the author, and which St. Thomas Aquinas illuminates when he establishes that the principal thing in the New Law, wherein lies all its strength, is the Grace of the Holy Spirit, working in souls through Faith and Charity. If a new Christendom is to arise in human history, it will not be by means of the police and military of self-styled Christian States, whose bankruptcy modern history has seen; it will be through the strength of the New Law, by the power of the Gospel regenerating from within the temporal structures of the world. Every Christian awaits the coming of a truly Christian order to the world, of a State really and organically Christian, which openly professes Christianity. But history forces us to recognize that so long as the State is not Christian in its vital structures, and so long as the claim of the State to be Christian does not express the profound desire and exulting faith of the human persons composing it, the political State, ever threatened by the demoniac principalities of which St. Paul speaks, exteriorly professes Christianity only at the expense of Christianity itself. In this matter it can be said that the motto of your University, *Leges sine moribus vanae,* finds special application.

In truth, the very idea of a Christian State appears today as something very remote. The new forms of State confronting Europe are totalitarian types claiming for themselves the messianic love due only to God, and having only one aim: to annihilate religion in the world or to pervert it in depth of souls, at times while pretending to defend it. Recently, on going through a commentary on the Apocalypse, I read that according to the well-known scholar, Dom Calmet, anti-Christ, "having assembled an immense army, will overthrow all the kingdoms of the world under the pretext of liberating peoples from tyranny and reëstablishing religion." No matter when the man of iniquity will appear in human history, this remark of Dom Calmet enlightens us on the nature of the temptations to which the faithful will be exposed in times to come. It also shows the duty of vigilance and discernment imposed upon religious thought in dark ages. The best way that Christians can serve religion is not to intrust its fate to political or semi-political means, be they utilized with the most ardent zeal, or still less to oscillate between one demon and another, through a misapplication of the principle of the lesser evil; the best way is to bring forth in the substance of the world that Grace of the Holy Spirit in which lies the entire strength of the New Law—and to tell the world the truth. For after all, what men first expect of religion is not to make them happy, but to tell them the truth.

The Modern Trends in European Protestant Theology

By

JOSEPH L. HROMÁDKA, Ph.D.*

THE main trend of the modern Protestant theology in Europe after the first Great War may be characterized as a new and deeper understanding of the fundamental problems and motifs of the Christian faith and Church. After a long period of historical, sociological, psychological, and epistemological analysis of the Christian life, individual and corporate, came a reverse swing to the basic questions of the divine truth. Whereas the pre-war theology was interested in what happened, and how and why it happened, the post-war theology began, very soon, to ask what was the supreme norm and criterion of our religious experience and thought. A few illustrations will indicate more clearly what I have in mind.

I

The breakdown of theological liberalism and humanism opened the door to a new, more adequate understanding of the divine revelation. Theologians began to take it seriously. They returned to the classic periods of the Christian era to listen to the way in which the leading confessors and thinkers of the Church had been approaching and interpreting the eternal truth. And they realized that the Christian Church and theology, from the very beginning of their existence, have been living by obedience and loyalty to the revealed truth of God. The pre-war theology was more or less introspective, searching for lasting values within the human mind and soul, within individual and collective experience, within history and nature; the post-war theology turned its eyes and ears towards the

* Guest Professor of Philosophy of Religion and Christian Ethics, Princeton Theological Seminary; Former Professor of Systematic Theology, University of Prague.

voice of God, coming from above, from the other shore. The pre-war theology was more horizontally minded, the modern theology became vertically minded. The post-war theologians realized more definitely and clearly that God is God, and man is man, that God is by His very nature absolutely different from the created world. In the pre-war theology there was an unceasing and irrepressible tendency to discover the point where God and the world (including history, nature, and the human soul) meet. It either humanized God or deified man and the universe. Its idea of God did not transcend the idea of the universe or of the spiritual life. The revelation was interpreted in terms of aesthetic, moral, or mystical experience. The modern theology radically altered the approach: *Revelatio Dei* means what it says. It is neither the better self of man nor the self-expression of the universe. The revelation is the unexplainable voice and word of God Himself, it is a challenge, a judgment, a call that we have to listen to, to accept or to reject it— on our own responsibility. The revelation is the divine *either— or*, unescapable, sovereign, free, and majestic. In other words, the supreme criterion of our thought and action is God Himself, what He speaks and reveals about Himself and about man, what was witnessed by the Old and New Testaments.

II

If the revealed and revealing God is the only starting point and the basis and the criterion of our faith and life, what about our reason, our conscience and moral judgment, our sentiments and emotions? How far, if ever, can they be trusted and relied on in our search for the ultimate truth and for the supreme criterion of life? What about men and women who never heard of the God of Israel or of the Lord Jesus Christ, and whose honest search for what is true, good, and beautiful cannot be disputed? Here we are facing one of the crucial problems and discussions, still going on, of the post-war theology. Whatever the controversy of the present and coming days may reveal, the revelation will remain the central pillar of theology and faith. The problem is only how to avoid dangers of a morbid irrationalism and of an obscurantist ritualism, how to bar temptations of a dismal dehumanization of life, dehumanization which very frequently follows the derationalization of religion and thought.

III

One of the most important problems to be solved is the interrelation between the divine grace and the divine law. The post-war theology laid a new emphasis upon the gospel of grace, mercy and love. And rightly so. The detrimental consequences of a moralistic and rationalistic religion were too evident. As evident as the fruits of romantic sentimentalism. A new understanding of the divine grace and mercy as the real nature of God and of His revelation was one of the essential elements of the post-war theological generation. A revival of Luther was symptomatic for the post-war theology.

However, the history of Christian theology and the Church warns us not to forget the fact that the faith is not only a grateful, humble acceptance of the divine grace; that the faith is not only an attitude of outstretched empty hands receiving divine gifts of forgiveness and justification; the history teaches us that the faith is simultaneously an attitude of responsibility, obligation, and sacrifice. The Lord Jesus Christ, crucified and risen, being the mediator of grace and mercy, is the Sovereign and Supreme Ruler and King over all areas of human life. All created beings are responsible to him. There is no No man's land where an uncontrolled human dominion could be established. There is no one single area where the so-called laws of self-determination were entitled to rule without being subjected to the higher, supreme authority of Jesus Christ. There is no faith without responsibility; no forgiveness of sins without obligation; no spiritual joy without loyalty and allegiance to the Lord of our life; there is no Savior without being the King of kings.

In other words, the discussion between Luther and Calvin must be going on, until the unity of the Old and New Covenants is reëstablished. Luther without Calvin and John Wesley might become an awful danger for Christian responsibility.

IV

Modern theology realized the enormous problem of the unity of Church, of the *Una Sancta*. It involved the breakdown of sectarian self-complacency and narrow-mindedness, a new, more constructive, approach to different historical forms of Christianity. Instead of controversy, antagonism, and polemics, a new theological attitude of mutual learning and listening, of sharing and understanding has taken place. Nobody who understands the substance of the Christian faith can, without scruples, justify the divisions of the Body of Christ and can be deaf as to the creed: *Credo unam, sanctam, catholicam, apostolicam ecclesiam.* For centuries there had been no such earnest and constructive encounter between Protestants and Catholics of all types as we were witnessing in the post-war period of Christian theology. The very essence and nature of the Church became one of the most important problems. What is the Church? A sacramental Body of Christ? A mystical communion of saints? A fellowship of sinners justified by and through the death and victory of Christ? A brotherhood of men and women in the service of Christ? An army of soldiers of Christ pledging their allegiance to the divine Lord and fighting against the forces of darkness and wickedness?

On an adequate solution of this problem depends largely the future, not only of organized Christianity, but of the secular life as well.

V

The modern theology has realized the fact that our civilization is at stake, and that all the essential heritage of the Christian history is in a great peril. And it recognized its own tremendous responsibility for this situation. The theology cannot evade and escape the question as to what ought to be foundation of our life outside the Church. Very likely the civilization is breaking down because we theologians have not done what was our mission and obligation. Apparently we have distorted the very essence of the divine truth, thus depriving civilization of its living and sustaining power.

The post-war theology begins to establish a new philosophy of history and civilization, a philosophy rooted in the fundamental message of the Gospel. As over against the pre-war theology, the new theology points to the central pillars of faith as being central pillars of our civilization.

The faith in creation is a barrier against pessimistic nihilism and rude naturalism.

The faith in the incarnation is a barrier against modern relativism and the mood of spectatorship.

The faith in the resurrection of Christ as a challenge to the sceptical mentality of indifference and carelessness.

The faith in the ultimate Judgment as a basis of creative earnestness and moral vigor—a continuous protest against any kind of monism obscuring and obliterating the definite line between good and evil, truth and falsehood, right and wrong, holiness and wickedness.

The faith in Christ, the supreme Lord, as barrier against any kind of totalitarianism.

The post-war theology has chosen a new (and still old) gallery of teachers and leaders. Whereas the old theology tried to adjust itself to the philosophical thinkers, the new theology goes in another direction. It does not minimize the greatness of Kant and Comte, Hegel and William James; however, it is oriented essentially towards the men of faith: St. Augustine and St. Anselm, St. Thomas and Erasmus, Luther and Calvin. The old struggle is going on: Who is the best or the most reliable interpreter of the Christian revelation? But it is a struggle with weapons which are far more appropriate than were the weapons of philosophical systems.

We are living in a terrific crisis. However, this crisis is a great challenge for us. If we theologians are faithful to the divine truth, we might be once credited with bringing good news and remedy to unhappy humanity.

Modern Trends in Catholic Theology

By

WILLIAM J. McGARRY, S.J., S.T.D., Lic., S.S.*

A UNIVERSITY is a forum where truth is sought, discussed, propagated; it is an arena where the character of youth is trained by absorbing truths concerning origin, birth, life, conduct, death, and all existence; it is a treasure-house where the learning and good example of the past is reflected in the erudition and good lives of the corps of professors; it is a sanctuary over which hovers the cloud of glory—of culture, religion, tradition, history, patriotism—and all walk in its illumination. As a human institution it does not always reach all its ideals; its success is graded. But when its victories are numerous, its achievements marked and its ideals safeguarded, it impels men to admire it and wish it well. On the ground of the merits of the University of Pennsylvania, I justly laud its good works of the past and present, and I sincerely wish it true advancement in its works of the future.

With the approval of the Committee which arranged the Symposium my topic is narrowed to a discussion of "Modern Trends in Catholic Theology." This is done on the ground of familiarity, even though limited, with the field of Catholic theology. Further, while it is desirable and necessary briefly to contrast the viewpoints of Catholic theology and that of others, I will follow the path of positive exposition rather than combat those whose views differ from my own.

Reflection upon the origin, direction, control, and evaluation of modern Catholic theological trends suggests a proper division of this paper. For the trend of any current thought is detectable because of the assumptions of philosophy and reason which underlie, inspire, and guide it. Thus, obviously, if one plumps for extinction after death and denies a soul during life, all talk of religious salvation is futile twaddle. Again, a larger controlling factor is one's theological viewpoint. If this

---

* Editor, *Theological Studies,* New York City.

27

negatives completely the supernatural and relegates all revelation and miracles to the class of mythical entities, obviously
the resultant theology will be at best some form of sociological
humanism. Or, if the controlling theological factor is a partial
or plenary, imposed or eclectic, opinion on revelation, the
effect of the viewpoint is found in very divergent theological
conclusions. Hence, doctrinal discussion in the Catholic Church
has a larger field of development than it has in the orthodox
Protestant theology because of the Protestant norm of exclusive
biblical authority. To the Catholic theologian apostolic tradition is also a source of definable doctrines.

Thirdly, the trend of any given systematic theology is to be
found in the historical and apologetic viewpoint adopted
therein. Here the transition occurs from the realm of reason
and nature to that of faith and supernature—a difficult step,
one will say, but not an impossible one. And, since all truth
derives from God, infinite truth, presumably the truth of reason and that of faith, will be complementary and not opposed,
cumulative and not mutually destructive, harmonizable and
not contradictory.

Finally the trend of theological thought (practice is the topic
of another part of the Symposium) is to be seen in the doctrines
actually discussed in our modern period. On these I will remark,
even when treating of the three topics above; in the main part
of this paper I will dwell more fully on particular doctrines
since they belong most properly to the subject assigned me.
They are, however, intelligible only in the light of the above-
named fundamental viewpoints upon which necessarily we
must dwell in a brief preliminary fashion. Brevity indeed has
its advantages; yet it compels omissions. I will try to heed the
warning of the Latin poet and will hope not to be too obscure
while I labor to be brief.

Catholic theology welcomes, as a remote control, the truths
of reason. The word "welcome" is used advisedly. For sane
philosophy and common sense do not consider the mind
shackled when it possesses truth; such possession is liberty—
liberty from error and ignorance. Really, there is a great freedom gained for the mind once it acquires a body of truths.
One is free to go on. And we mark that mankind adopts this
view with respect to many of its mental pursuits; but somehow,
in theology especially, but in ethics and psychology as well, the

new generations are tempted to throw out the acquisitions of the past, and only too often after superficial examination of them. In my opinion this accounts for the mesmeric influence which Immanuel Kant has exercised over modern minds. How many agnostics have really studied the pages on which Kant rejected the arguments of rational theism, and if you name a thousand, then one may ask how many of these have turned to a thorough analytical study of the arguments for God's existence which Kant treated so lightly.

The remote control exercised over theological thought functions actually in nearly every theological axiom and thesis. I may name, therefore, only those philosophical viewpoints of larger import. Deep rooted in all Catholic theology is a triple dualism of reason—that of God and creatures, that of spirit and matter, that of right and wrong. Dualism implies distinction, and thus immediately pantheism is rejected because God and creation are two, not one; materialism is rejected because our spirit is not like the body, subject to corruption; and amorality is ruled out because, through law and conscience, man's free will is guided to an immortal destiny. Yet dualism does not imply lack of contact. Spirit and matter form one person, and the ego has one destiny. God and creation are linked, and all the relations of the creature subject to its God and Master are set up both in the matter of knowing as well as in that of free action.

To illustrate: Certainly a trend in modern Catholic theology is its opposition to Communistic ideology in regard of atheistic views as well as of those determining the relation of man to the State. The opposition stems from the theses which belong to reason and philosophy which have been accepted and defended by the Church, namely, the right of private property, the existence and dignity of God, the personality and destiny of free, rational creatures who are not pawns and chattels of an Hegelian monster-state, but sons of God as well as free citizens. On such points there is in reason no dispute. Hence, in handling such themes, the Church does not enter the arena to debate with Communists or dictators; she announces to the world the truths of reason and warns her children from engaging upon the aimless task of searching grains of truth in false ideologies. For this reason the Church often may seem too apodictic and narrow-minded to some. This is but her consciousness of her strength in her acquired truths and her confident and fearless fulfillment of her mission to preach and safeguard truth.

The body of truths which reason possesses is, of course, a possession common to the Catholic Church and to all others who will follow the rigid paths of logic in searching out truth. But there are, in the Catholic view, truths beyond reason. That is, truths which unaided reason cannot attain, such as the doctrine that God is one in nature and three in persons. In this case the fact of a Trinity is beyond the reach of reason, and even after being told the fact, our mind cannot see positively and plenarily how it can be. It can only say—well, after all, nature and person are not necessarily one, even though every human nature I know is a person and vice versa; if God says that He is three in person, this must be, for He is God and I am creature; He knows the infinite reaches of all truth; I have but a finite mind and presumably there is a field of truth outside its purview.

But if there is thus a transition to a vaster field of truth in which reason does not lead but must reasonably follow, how does Catholic theology breach the gap, and what effect has its manner of doing so on its current theology? It makes this transit by reason and history. It accepts the fact that God is God and man is creature. It then argues: If God has spoken to man, His creature, then man must accept and obey fully the message, whatever be its content and import, whatever be its cost or pleasure, whatever be its manner of promulgation, its mode of procedure, its instrument of evangelization.

That much reason makes plain. But this thesis of reason includes a mighty "if." Has God spoken to man? That is a matter of historical investigation, a matter still within the reach of human reason. On *historical* grounds Catholic theology accepts the fact that God has spoken a definite message to mankind, principally through His Son, Jesus Christ. The establishing of this historical thesis, the running down of the thousand minutiae, implications and features of it, the answering of the hundreds of modern objections to it take nearly one year, the first, in a Catholic seminary course at the rate of seven or eight lectures a week. I omit a development of this Catholic apologetic, and pass on to illustrate how the apologetic viewpoint controls modern trends in Catholic theology.

First, about the turn of this present century the movement

called Modernism arose through an erroneous and unwonted admiration of and subservience to the inadequate philosophy of Naturalism. Modernism was indeed a bundle of all heresies, but its worst features were apparent in its attack on God. With Kant it removed God from the field of intelligence to that of emotions or will. With German Rationalism it doubted or denied Christ's divinity. Thus as a trend it disregarded the control of philosophy and reason and bred agnostics, and yielded before the attack of Naturalism and bred skeptics who still called themselves Christians. From reasonably argued philosophy and apologetics the orthodox counter-current originated, and through vigorous thought and action Modernism was expelled from the Church. Its protagonists are still hailed in some quarters outside the Church as champions of reason. Among us they are regarded as having suffered from a surprising inferiority complex in the face of Naturalistic Rationalism.

Again, from the apologetic viewpoint adopted in Catholicism a trend is notable in the modern Catholic biblical research. This is in reaction against the historical skepticism which has discredited the Bible in such wide quarters, even affecting Protestant scholars who might be expected to be champions of an inspired and inerrant scripture. The counter-trend to this historical skepticism is seen first in the greater emphasis given to scriptural history and criticism in Catholic writings and studies. Secondly, in the establishment of the Biblical Commission. This is a Pontifical commission of five cardinals to which is attached a body of some forty consultors, all of them experts in biblical studies, and, incidentally, representatives of the conservative and liberal views in the myriad disputable points of biblical science. The Commission sets forth authoritatively, though not with a claim to infallible pronouncement, viewpoints which Catholic theologians adopt. Among other points proposed during the last thirty years mention may be made of the decrees wherein it is stated that Matthew, Mark, Luke, and John are the authors of the Gospels traditionally assigned to them; that Moses is the author of the Pentateuch; that the historical statements of the first three chapters of Genesis are to be accepted as revealed history and truth.

We pass on to a consideration of the trends in Catholic theology itself. Theology as a science presupposes a reasonable philosophy and a rationally argued apologetic; it discusses as well *from its own standpoint* many propositions of the pre-theological sciences. Thus, philosophy can prove an immortal spiritual soul; theology also holds this proposition; philosophy argues to it through many steps by an analysis of universal or generalized ideas; theology states that God has said man's soul is immortal. Thus reason and faith sustain the same proposition, but each in its own way. To illustrate again, Gospel skeptics believe that Christ died; they do so by an assent of human faith. A Catholic too believes this, believes it because God has revealed it through the Scripture and tradition—and this is Divine Faith; he also believes it on human faith, if, apologetically, he studies the Gospels as history apart from their quality of being divinely inspired writings.

But while theology thus adds another and separate motive for many propositions of reason, it is concerned properly with those propositions as revealed. It is therefore as a scientific procedure an investigation of the contents of Divine Revelation, an analysis of the propositions to which man assents on the ground that God has revealed His message. God's message is contained in the written Scriptures and in the teaching of the Apostles, or tradition. Since that message is conveyed to fallible men and is subject to perversion, corruption, and misinterpretation, Catholic theology claims both as a matter of historical apologetics and as a part of revelation, that God through Christ set up an infallible guide, defender, and interpreter of revelation in His Church and in His Vicar, the successor of Peter. If God commanded men down to the end of time to accept under penalty of salvation or damnation what the Apostles taught, then God must have set up an instrument to safeguard that teaching. Else, under pain of Hell, God might be commanding men to accept error—a patent absurdity.

From these viewpoints it might seem to follow that Catholic theology is reduced to cataloguing the propositions of revelation. It does this, but this is the simplest part of its task. A proposition obviously has an explicit content; there are also implicit statements contained in the proposition; there are related propositions; there are inferences, both obvious and subtle; there are presuppositions. Scientific theology deals with all these. The implicit content of a revealed proposition may become clear only after long discussion and controversy. I may illustrate this from the history of the doctrine of the Immaculate Conception, that is, the dogma that Mary, Mother of God, was exempted from original sin, though a daughter of Adam. In passing, I note that this doctrine is not to be confused with an entirely distinct doctrine that Mary bore Christ virginally, that is, without congress of man in conception and without rupture of virginal membranes in delivery.

In the case of the doctrine of the Immaculate Conception, Scripture and tradition stated Mary's sinlessness, and placed her even above the Angels. Theology investigated the extent of this sinlessness. For several centuries this problem occupied men's minds. Was Mary's sinlessness so complete as even to include her immunity from original sin? Was this proposition implicitly averred in the statement of her sinlessness? It was not clear to many great theologians. Saints Bernard, Bonaventure and others, even Saint Thomas Aquinas, are named as doubting it. Their difficulty lay in the fact that this dogma seemed to mean Mary's exemption from Christ's redemption. When Scotus proposed that it did not, when he showed that Mary was redeemed, not by the reparation of loss actually suffered, but by prevention through the merits of Christ of a loss that threatened every child of Adam, the light began to be perceived more clearly. When it was seen that her utter sinlessness perennially proclaimed did not contravene other doctrines, the implicit proposition was seen to be contained in the statement of the utter stainlessness of the Virgin. Yet four centuries elapsed before the dogma, held and safeguarded by theologians following Scotus, was defined as an article of faith. I take this example from the theology of Mary, from Mariology, because when I come to mark out modern trends in Catholic theology, something more will be said on Mariology.

It remains now to describe some of the actual trends of modern Catholic theology. In general these trends originate from two sources, one within the Church, the other outside it. Theological currents due to causes within the Church are the result of her own restless mental and devotional energy. To both of these is due in recent years the theological emphasis on such topics as the Mystical Body of Christ, on several doctrines affecting Our Lady, on several points affecting the Blessed Sacrament and the Sacrifice of the Mass. Moreover, certain liturgical and canonical movements are noteworthy in modern Catholicism. Movements due to causes outside the Church are generally reactions against ideologies which attack the Church's received doctrines. Mention has been made already of the anti-communistic stand taken in modern Catholicism, as well as that against naturalistic rationalism which denies all the super-natural, revelation, miracles, and the Divinity of Christ. It is left only to take notice of the anti-evolutionary trend in Catholic theology.

In its aspects which are antithetic to Catholic theology, Evolution is a philosophy which plumps for a naturalistic and exclusive continuity, that is, it postulates a cause *within* a given system for any effect. Thus it sees man's soul as an end-product of the multitudinous and infinitesimal advances of the feeblest life manifestations of protozoic vital activity; it regards Christianity as a natural effect and an end-product and an amalgam of religious tendencies found in Judaism and Hellenism; it states that human ethics are animal instincts raised to the stature of laws and conscience; it thinks man, body and soul, is a product of evolving animals.

Against these propositions Catholic theologians have been busy in recent years. They point out that the basic thesis of continuity is false and unproven, simply because God the Lord cannot in principle be assumed never to interfere in His world. Reasonably they argue that matter cannot evolve into spirit; hence God intervenes at every creation of a human soul. Again, free responsible men are moral beings; their ethics are not polished customs of non-moral animals. Thirdly, Christianity originated out of the supernatural intervention of God through the Incarnation of the Son of God; it is not a syncretistic mixtum-gatherum of Jesus, Paul, Judaism, and paganism.

On the evolution of man's body a further word may be said. Here theology comes in contact with data supplied by biology, prehistory, and anthropology. Truths derived from these sciences are welcome to Catholic theologians; long experience, however, has taught the Church to distrust, not science, but the exaggerated claims of many scientists. In principle, where the data of other sciences touch matters dealt with in theology, a harmonization is always possible. For natural and revealed truths stem from one Divine Source. In this particular case, according to the statements of the most careful scientists, it has not been proved definitely that man's body evolved from that of a brute, even though scientists rightly point out the magnitude of their evidence of continuity. On the other hand, the commonly accepted meaning read out of Genesis is that the formation of man's body was due to a specific Divine intervention. Confronted with an apparent conflict between the hypotheses of science and the commonly accepted theological view (be it noted, not an article of faith) the Catholic theologian follows the principle accepted since Saint Augustine's time and formulated by Pope Leo XIII: one is not to withdraw from a proposition of long standing which has been commonly accepted in the Church until the data of science are so well established as to invite reconsideration and reformulation of the traditional opinion. In the case of the evolution of man's body, the question concerns an interpretation of Genesis of which as yet there is no exegesis officially and infallibly given. The question also involves dogmas which are defined, and immutably defined, namely, those which proclaim man's inheritance of original sin through a descent from a single parent, Adam. In sum, in this matter the Catholic theologian is invited to accept what is true and proven in any science when it *is* true and proven, just as the Catholic anthropologist and biologist are invited to pursue with absolute honesty and rigorous logic their scientific researches.

We may now turn to the theological topics which are the offspring of the thought and devotion of the Church in our day and are the object of study and research.

The first of these is the doctrine of the Mystical Body of Christ. There is not now the time to develop this topic at length. Suffice it to say that if we look on the State and its citizens as a moral unit, a reality in the moral order, the Church as the Mystical Body of Christ is this and more. It is a reality, but a reality of the supernatural order. How it is real, how its members are related to its Head, Christ, how far it extends, whom it comprises and how, are questions discussed among us and still discussible. The brief saying that the Mystical Body of Christ is the extension in time and space of the Christ of Nazareth and Calvary may not be simple, but it is probably the best formulation of a doctrine which is, after all, a mystery, and it will not be made entirely plain to us on this earth. In order not to trespass on the topic of modern practical trends in theology, I merely remark that the newly energized liturgical movement within the Catholic Church has been stimulated by the doctrine of the Mystical Body. Moral, ascetical, and devotional life also benefit from the emphasis placed on this dogma.

Two principal topics in the theology of the Virgin Mother of God are now discussed among us. They are, first, that Mary, in body and soul, was assumed into heaven; and secondly, that Mary, Mother of God, is, under Christ, the mediatrix of all graces. Neither of these propositions is an article of faith. The doctrine of Mary's assumption is now called "definable" among Catholic theologians, that is, it is contained implicitly in view of Our Lady's privilege which is the heritage of the past tradition of the Church and ultimately derives from the Apostles. This doctrine means that the Mother of God died, that her soul and body were separated, were united again, and that Mary, in risen form, was assumed into heaven just as Christ ascended thither from Olivet, and as we shall rise, if saved, on the Last Day.

The other doctrine that Mary is the mediatrix of all graces is now in the stage of controversy. That is, ideas are yet to be clarified, more precise formulations are to be achieved, certain difficulties, objections, and obscurities are to be cleared up, the extent of Mary's place in the work of redemption, the relation of her divine maternity to her place in the redemption, her relations to men, the co-heirs of the Redeemer, all these need further illumination and determination. On these questions Catholic theologians are at present divided and probably will be divided for some decades to come. In the meantime, the output of articles, brochures, and treatises on both of the above features of Marian theology is enormous.

A renewed emphasis on the doctrine dealing with the Blessed Sacrament is the result, as far as practice is concerned, of the impetus given to daily Communion by the decree of Pope Pius X. In respect of theory, the writings of Father de la Taille, S.J., were the occasion of a renewed interest in theories concerning the Holy Sacrifice of the Mass. In the sixteenth century the denials which emanated from the Protestant theologians occasioned the formulation in articles of faith of the Church's century-old doctrines that Christ was present in the Blessed Sacrament, Body, Blood, Soul, and Divinity, that this Presence followed upon a transubstantiation of the elements, and that this transubstantiation occurred in the Consecration of the

Mass, which was a true sacrifice and one with the Sacrifice of the Cross.

How the Mass was truly a sacrifice was a question which vexed and still vexes Catholic theologians. The doctrine asserting the fact was always clear; the explanations differed. All admitted that one and the same Victim was offered, that the priest offered the Victim ministerially for Christ, that the number of separate offerings of the Victim increased each day. Two principal explanations of the problem were offered. One school held that a mystical immolation sufficed to constitute the Mass a real sacrifice. Hence, there was one real death and immolation on Calvary, only a mystical and repeated immolation in the Mass. An opposite school held that to have a real sacrifice, the quality of victimhood must here and now in each Mass be assumed by Christ. They saw the Victim endue this quality of victimhood because Christ in the Mass is present without the visible accompaniment of the qualities He has in His risen Body in heaven. To these opinions a third view, not new but allegedly the bearing of patristic thought on the Eucharist, was added by Father de la Taille. It held that for the reality of a sacrifice no real immolation is here and now required. What is required is a real victim in the hands of an offerer. Thus, as Christ at the supper offered the sacrifice of a victim to be immolated on the morrow, so priests now offer the sacrifice of a victim immolated on the yesterday of Calvary. Further, this present offering in the Mass repeats dramatically and reënacts mystically and in an unbloody manner the bloody Sacrifice of Calvary. None of these theories has been raised to the dignity of an article of faith. In the seminaries one or other of the three views with minor modifications is being taught.

Mention must be made here of the codification of the Church's Canon Law. The New Code, consisting of some twenty-four hundred brief canons, was promulgated at Pentecost, 1918. It is an epitome of the vast mass of Canon Law which had been developing from the days of the Church's early conversion of the Roman Law into a systematical corpus of canons to govern her own procedure. I pause only to mention in passing the praise of this recent codification which lawyers outside as well as within the Church have given. Hundreds of canonists co-operated in this work, but principal among them was the most eminent canonist of our day, the former Papal Secretary of State, Pietro Cardinal Gasparri.

Finally, in recent years, an increased interest among Catholic theologians has been aroused in matters touching the Eastern Churches. This renewed interest began with the efforts of the Holy See to reunite to her the groups of Christians long separated from Rome. The efforts have succeeded in no small measure. Due to this procedure of the Popes, theologians and historians have occupied themselves with the doctrines and history of the several schisms. In all this recent study an irenic note is definitely sounded. In matters of doctrine there is one path which all must follow, for the message of God's revelation is one which may not be tampered with; but in matters of liturgy and Canon Law, the Eastern Churches are to follow their own tradition as the Latin West follows its own. Unity of faith does not mean unity in liturgical and canonical details.

If, thus, the Catholic Church is ecumenically minded as her note of Catholicity demands, possibly the question occurs to your minds concerning her attitude to the recent ecumenical movement which is so emphatically an interest of the non-Catholic Western Churches. The Catholic Church has been accused of intolerance and pride, because she does not enter the arena of doctrinal discussion but awaits the submission of those whom she names heretics. Let me explain her attitude briefly. She holds that God has revealed a message which men must accept. She also holds that she is the interpreter and guardian of that message. She can no more discuss whether or not she will hold and preach, let us say, a Trinity or Christ's Real Presence in the Eucharist, than a mathematical faculty can open for discussion and dissent the proposition that two and two are four or that an equilateral triangle has three equal sides and angles. When God speaks, the Catholic Church says in effect, human discussion is futile and human compromise is a crime.

Again, the Church is sure that Christ set up a kingdom which is a monarchy. Can she, therefore, enter a hall where the assumption is a denial of this, where hierarchy and orders are neglected in favor of making a democracy out of a kingdom? One may disagree that Christ set up a monarchy, for all His use of the word "kingdom," and His appointment of Peter and the Apostles perennially to govern the Church's Faith, morals, and procedure. Very well, one may disagree with the Church, but one must admit the Church's rightness and correctness in acting logically according to her own convictions.

This topic leads me to some conclusory remarks upon modern trends in Catholic theology. Roads of divergence from the trends noticeable in other systems of theology are discernible. When a comparison is made between the faith and beliefs of other Western Churches and those of the Catholic Church during the last four centuries, inevitably one is forced to recognize that non-Catholic theology has suffered a liberalization which is due to Deistic philosophy and its modern progeny, Naturalistic Rationalism. In the Catholic Church this philosophy has not gained a prominent place; the brief episode of Modernism stamped it out. The doctrines which we hold now are those held previously—and especially has Catholic theology held to the Nicene Creed, which is certainly not professed in its full unequivocal sense by theologians and writers of other churches.

Yet in other matters we may note currents of thought in which Catholic and non-Catholic theology are proceeding, if not in the same path, at least in similar directions.

Mention may be made of two tendencies. Within Catholicism I have mentioned the doctrine of the Mystical Body of Christ. Outside it I note a much greater emphasis on the sociological aspects of religion. Secondly, within Catholicism the striving for unity is always strong. "Preach the Gospel to every creature" is a command laid upon the Church. Hence, any ecumenical movement is of interest, though non-Catholic opinion on procedure and means differs very radically from that of the Church. However, unity will never be without the strong yearning for union and hence the Church's daily prayer, as Christ prayed, "That they all may be one, as Thou, Father, in me, and I in Thee."

The trends of modern Catholic theology embrace and forward the desires of Christ and all good Christians for unity. For any genuine theological tendency in Catholicism has as its purpose unity of doctrine, unity of action, unity of spirit, and unity of faith.

Unchanging Ethics in a Changing World

By

JOHN A. RYAN, D.D., S.T.D., LL.D., Litt.D.*

By transporting slightly the phrasing of this title and changing one word, we could get a topic no less interesting and timely than the one before us. Thus modified, the title would read: "Changing Ethics in a Confused World." It would provide not only a topic to be discussed but a thesis to be defended. It would suggest a relation of cause and effect; for the confusion in the world today is in large measure the effect of changes in ethical theories and practices over a period of many decades. However, that is not the subject assigned to me. Whatever attention it receives will be only incidental or implicit.

As a science, ethics deals with human actions under the aspect of right and wrong. As a system, ethics lays down the principles and rules of right conduct. Some ethical treatises are merely descriptive, exhibiting the moral codes that have been accepted or practised by races, groups, or individuals; others are mainly normative, defining and defending the principles and rules of conduct that are regarded as right. In this paper I shall deal with ethics as a system of principles and rules, and shall defend that particular system which I believe to be in accord with natural reason and Christian revelation.

In his Encyclical letter "On the Function of the State in the Modern World," Pope Pius XII declares:

> Before all else, it is certain that the radical and ultimate cause of the evils which We deplore in modern society is the denial and rejection of a universal norm of morality as well for individual and social life as for international relations; We mean the disregard, so common nowadays, and the forgetfulness of the natural law itself, which has its foundation in God, Almighty Creator and Father of all, supreme and absolute Lawgiver, all-wise and just Judge of human actions.

* Professor of Social Ethics, National Catholic School of Social Service; Director, Department of Social Action, National Catholic Welfare Conference.

Time is wanting for a comprehensive description of the evils which the Holy Father deplores in modern society. Nor is it necessary for our present purpose. Nevertheless, some of the worst of our present-day evils provide us with a significant approach to the consideration of our topic. They constitute a large part of our changing world, have been brought about mainly by false ethics, and can be removed only by a return to sound ethics.

The two most conspicuous and most devastating groups of evils now afflicting society are found in family life and in political life. In the former, the principal evils are divorce and the declining birth rate. The number of divorces per thousand marriages is greater in the United States than in any other country in the world, with the possible exception of Japan. I do not need to describe, nor even to enumerate, the socially and morally destructive effects and implications of this scandalous situation, as regards conjugal fidelity, self-discipline and family discipline, domestic happiness, the nurture of children, the practice of altruism, and the training of men, women, and children for good citizenship. Our birth rate has fallen so far that within a very few years deaths will equal births and the country will be face to face with an inevitably declining population. No person who is competent to pass judgment upon the subject can regard this prospect with complacency. Once the population has begun to diminish, the trend can be checked only by heroic measures which are not now within the range of probability. So long as the decline continues, it will mean progressive national decadence, with the ultimate result of either national extinction or conquest by an alien nation or an alien race.

In political life the great menace today is Totalitarianism— "an ugly word for an ugly thing"—as it was recently called by Cardinal Hinsley, Archbishop of Westminster. Whether the Totalitarian state professes the principles of Communism, Nazism, or Fascism makes little practical difference. All three of these monstrous systems deny and disregard the dignity of the human person, the rights and liberties of the individual, freedom of speech, of education, of the press, representative government, adequate opportunity to acquire and to use property, and even a minimum degree of economic freedom. In a word, the Totalitarian state compels the individual to be totally subject to it, in all his activities, beliefs, and relations. This is the internal or domestic aspect of Totalitarianism. In their external relations, the Totalitarian states act upon the principle that the end justifies the means, therefore that in their dealings with other states they may and ought to use unlimited force, cunning, treachery, and lies.

What is the bearing of ethics upon these deplorable conditions? In attempting to answer this question, I shall confine myself to two considerations: first, the inadequateness of false ethics; second, the saving possibilities of sound ethics.

Obviously it will be impossible, within the limits of this paper, to deal with all the systems of ethics which have contributed either positively or negatively to the production and persistence of the evils sketched above. Therefore I propose to present the two types of ethical doctrine which have for many years and still are most widely held by those who have rejected the old morality. By the old morality, I mean the moral system of Christianity. Men who accepted this system regarded the moral law as a Divine enactment. Right was right, wrong was wrong, good was good, bad was bad—because these concepts were thought to reflect the Divine Reason and to express the Divine decrees. God was looked upon as the foundation, the source, the guarantor, and the sanctioner of the entire moral code. All these ethical beliefs, all this ethical teaching, was laid down, explained, and enforced by living, active organizations. The answer to the question, "How ought I live?" was clearly and authoritatively presented in the teaching of organized religion.

The two types of doctrine which have been substituted by ethical thinkers for the Christian system may be conveniently distinguished by prefixing to them the epithets "idealistic" and "hedonistic." Neither of them presents anything new. In essence both are as old as ethical discussion; both can be found in the writings of the ancient Greeks.

As fairly typical of a large group of idealistic ethical principles and proposals, I would cite those offered by Walter Lippmann. A few years ago he produced a very readable and in some parts a very thoughtful book, entitled *A Preface to Morals*. In the first part he describes the decay of the old morality and the unsatisfactory conditions resulting. In the second and third parts he develops a moral system which he recommends to those who no longer accept a moral code based upon religion.

The fundamental principle of his proposed system he calls "high religion" and defines its dominant quality as "disinterestedness." Despite his attractive language, his argument is unconvincing. The man who has thrown off authoritative morality and its sanctions will raise the old, old question:

Why should I act disinterestedly when I am persuaded that I shall get more happiness or larger satisfactions out of life by acting selfishly? Disinterested actions may in some circumstances be necessary in order to obtain greater satisfaction later on, but I see no reason why I should make a habit of disinterestedness when I know that it will involve me in many unpleasant experiences. I am willing to consult experience in order to learn what actions are desirable, but you must permit me to make my own choice of the desirable. Exercising this liberty, I do not find that uniform disinterestedness is desirable, either as an end or as a means. I want to be happy, and I do not believe that I can attain happiness if I always follow disinterestedness.

Neither Mr. Lippmann nor anyone else can refute this argument. The average person who has rejected the old morality cannot be persuaded that disinterested conduct will bring him the maximum of happiness, as he understands happiness. No doubt a few generous souls will accept Mr. Lippmann's principle because they are so constituted, but the problem facing him is to find a rule of conduct which will appeal to the vast majority. Mr. Lippmann's and all similar versions of idealistic ethics may be summarily dismissed as impractical and futile. While they cannot be held directly responsible for the evil practices noted above, they have contributed thereto indirectly, in so far as they have diverted men's minds from a consideration of sound ethical principles.

The hedonistic type of ethical doctrine is not only futile and impractical but, in one form or another, it is directly responsible for the deplorable evils affecting family life and political life. Hedonistic ethics places the highest good of man in earthly happiness. But happiness is always relative to some person or persons. It is not an absolute and independent entity. Even when one aims at the happiness of another in preference to one's own, one is seeking the happiness of a person, not happiness in the abstract. For the believer in a future life, happiness is a sufficiently compelling end; such a person is thinking of his own final happiness. But happiness on earth rests upon an entirely different basis. It must be conceived either in relation to one's self or to society. In the former case, each person will determine for himself whether the happiness that he seeks shall be selfish or unselfish, or a combination of both. Serious and competent moralists realize that the vast majority of persons who deliberately pursue their own happiness degenerate into mere seekers of selfish pleasures. Hence the proponents of the happiness morality would have the individual refrain from pursuing his own happiness or pleasure when these conflict with the happiness of society or mankind. Surely this is illogical. Since happiness is an individual matter, why should one person deprive himself of it for another person? or for another group of persons? or for an entire nation? or even for a whole race?

These questions are not adequately answered by the reply that today many millions of men in at least three countries are subordinating personal happiness to the interests of the race, to the state or to conceptions of national power and glory. Some of these millions are acting under compulsion; others are hoping that they will ultimately find individual benefit or pleasure or happiness, while still other millions are temporarily obsessed by such abstractions as racial purity and superiority, the glory of the nation or the triumph of the proletariat.

The illusiveness of the hedonistic morality is sufficiently evident in the condition of mind of those who have already given it a trial. I refer to the generation that has approached or reached maturity since the World War. Large numbers of this generation have been in rebellion against the religion and the moral code of their parents, and have substituted therefore the tenets and the implications of the happiness morality; yet, as Mr. Lippmann points out, they are already in a condition of "disillusionment with their own rebellion." No competent observer will dispute this generalization. The persons who have boldly and consistently adopted the happiness morality are neither happy nor satisfied.

So much for the false systems of ethics and what they have done to change our world for the worse. Inasmuch as I did not choose the title of this address, I do not know all its intended implications. Possibly it is supposed to suggest that a changing world requires a changing ethics; that changes in the dominant practices and beliefs of a social group indicate a need for corresponding changes in ethical principles and codes. For myself, I reject all such assumptions. In order to be acceptable, suitable, and objectively true, an ethical code must be adapted to and in conformity with essential human nature. Man is still what he was defined to be by Aristotle, a rational animal. Despite whatever evolution he has undergone, his nature remains essentially what it was when God breathed into him "a living soul." Until man becomes essentially other than a rational animal, for example, an angel or a gorilla, he will require the same system of ethical rules that have served and suited him throughout his entire earthly history. To be sure, the rules will have to be applied, as they always have been applied, differently in different circumstances and conditions, but their essential principles will remain eternally true and adequate.

According to all ethical systems, morally good conduct is that which is in accord with reason. Now the test of reasonableness in man's conduct is essentially the same as the test of propriety in the actions of any other being, whether sub-human or super-human: it is conformity with nature. Cows do not fly, nor do angels eat grass. In every case the norm and guide of proper actions and reasonable actions is nature. According to Webster's *International Dictionary*, nature is "the sum of the qualities and attributes which make a person or thing what it is, as distinct from others; its essential form or individual character." This, however, is a definition of essence rather than of nature. Aristotle's formulation is briefer, more precise, and more specific: "Nature is the essence of a thing considered as the principle or source of activities." In common language nature almost always connotes activity, operation. In man, as in other animals, nature is the proper norm of actions. Between man and the non-rational animals, there is, however, a fundamental difference with regard to the way in which nature and its authority are to be conceived. In brute animals all actions are *necessarily* in conformity with nature. They cannot be otherwise. In man all actions are necessarily proportionate to his physical and intellectual nature, but not all are in harmony with his moral nature. Every human act responds to some natural desire, is the expression of a natural capacity, but some human acts are in conflict with other capacities and needs of human nature; for example, the habitual use of narcotics, numerous other practices which are injurious to health, and those acts of sensual indulgence which cause intellectual degeneration. In other words, the exercise of some faculties in some circumstances interferes with the exercise of other faculties. Yet both sets of faculties are constituent elements of human nature and have valid claims to consideration.

The problem thus raised can be solved only by assuming a certain order, or hierarchy, among the faculties. Some faculties must be subordinated to others, and every faculty must be exercised consistently with the welfare of the whole man. Accordingly, the norm of conduct and the true basis of moral judgments may be formulated thus: rational nature adequately considered; that is, in its *constitution* and *essential relations*. Examining man's *constitution*, we find that the rational part is intrinsically higher than the animal part. The latter is merely an instrument. Its value is determined by its utility for the rational part and for the whole. In case of conflict between the rational faculties and the sense faculties, the former must be preferred. The sense faculties must be exercised in such a way as not to hinder the exercise and development of the rational faculties. From this principle we derive our moral condemnation of such acts as drunkenness and solitary unchastity.

The *essential relations* of rational nature are threefold: to a higher Being, to lower beings, and to equals. The first relation requires recognition, obedience, and worship rendered to God. The second authorizes man to use the lower creatures, animals, plants, and minerals, as mere instruments for his own welfare. The third relation connects the individual with his fellow men. It requires him to treat them as equals, as having the same intrinsic worth, the same nature, the same needs, and the same rights. They are always to be regarded as ends in themselves, never as mere instruments. From this relation follow the duties of charity, justice, veracity, and all the other virtues that are required by the various forms of human association.

With regard to the implications of the principle of equality for organized groups, I shall notice only one social organization. Since the State is in accord with and required by rational nature, it has a moral claim upon the loyalty and support of its members. But it is not an end in itself. It is but a means to the welfare of individuals. In times of grave danger to the community, it may properly require grave sacrifices from its members, but it may never use any of them as mere means to its assumed welfare. If it did so it would subordinate intrinsically sacred beings either to a mere abstraction or to a part, albeit a majority, of its members. The latter have no greater intrinsic worth than the persons whose rights have been ignored.

Thus conceived, rational nature constitutes a reasonable norm of conduct and a reasonable basis of objective moral judgments. It is consistent with all genuine human needs and human development. To be sure, it does not ensure uniform judgments on all the details of conduct. Some of the world's ablest thinkers have accepted this norm of conduct and the general principles which it involves, and yet have disagreed on many questions of practical application. However, this limitation affects every ethical system and, indeed, every practical science: witness the disagreements among authorities in medicine, economics, and politics.

In the foregoing exposition of the fundamental principle of ethics, the adequate norm of morality, the unfailing criterion of right conduct, the critical phrases are "intrinsically superior," and "intrinsic worth." Persons who reject this system, particularly those who cling to any form of hedonistic ethics, can object that the asserted "intrinsic" superiority and claims of the rational faculties, i.e., the intellect and the disinterested will, over the sense faculties are unproved, and indeed have no intelligible meaning; and that the "intrinsic" worth of the human person, with its implication that all persons are essentially equal, is likewise devoid of probative force and intelligibility. Perhaps the only semblance of empirical evidence that can be adduced for these concepts is the fact that few if any men have ever consistently and completely denied them in their individual actions and social relations. In a very large measure, the concepts of intrinsically higher faculties and the intrinsic dignity of the human person are accepted and supported by the common consent of mankind.

Nevertheless we must admit, and even insist, that these concepts are not susceptible of inductive demonstration. By observation we learn that the dome of the city hall is higher than the bootblack's stand on the first floor, but no amount of mere observation and induction will yield the conclusion that the rational faculties are higher than the animal faculties. By experience we know that scarce commodities have economic value, but no quantity or quality of experience will enable us to prove that men have intrinsic worth. The concepts and the propositions under consideration here belong to a different order of reality. If they are not self-evident they are as unsubstantial as the gossamer texture of a dream. They cannot be empirically proved any more than the principle of contradiction.

Similar statements are true of all other ethical systems. They all rest ultimately upon intuitions, or imagined intuitions. No one can inductively demonstrate that individual happiness, or social utility, or national welfare, or national power, or racial purity, constitutes the highest good for men to seek. Their ultimate intellectual basis is a species of faith.

Let us attempt to apply very briefly our ethical principles to the two groups of evils noticed at the beginning of this paper. Easy divorce and its deplorable consequences, the declining birth rate, its main cause and its numerous evil implications and results—are all contrary either to the intrinsic superiority of the higher faculties or to the intrinsic worth and essential equality of men, or to both. Totalitarianism, with all its tenets and works is condemned by the principles of intrinsic human worth, essential human equality, and the subordination of the state to human welfare. Unless we hold to these principles we cannot logically defend the rights of the individual, or the institutions of democracy.

In conclusion, I recur to the statement of the Holy Father which implies that the greatest need of our time is that "universal norm of morality," known as "the natural law, which has its foundation in God . . ." As many of you realize, it is the natural law that I have been attempting to construe, expound, and defend. All the principles and rules that I have set down are within the compass of natural reason. In theory, at least, they could all be derived from the natural law by an enlightened pagan. While most of the great minds of the ancient world knew and accepted the natural law, none of them, not even Plato or Sophocles or Cicero, developed it adequately or applied it comprehensively. That development and that appreciation has been the unique task and achievement of the authorized teachers of Christianity. The rejection of the natural law is mainly due to the departure from traditional Christian teaching. While the ethical principles and rules herein set forth are theoretically independent of Christianity, they are vitally dependent upon it in practice.

Finally, the intuitive concepts of the intrinsic order among the faculties, and the intrinsic worth and sacredness of the human person, are practically and logically dependent upon a belief in God. This is implied in the Pope's statement that the natural law has its "foundation in God." If I am asked how I know that my ethical intuitions are not an illusion, I reply that their existence in my mind and the clearness and power with which they impress me, cannot be adequately explained except on the ground that they are reflections of the mind of the Creator. The conviction that I am obliged to respect the intrinsic superiority of the higher faculties and the intrinsic dignity of the person, is a reflection of the Divine Will, while my intuitions of these truths and values are a reflection of the Divine Reason. God is at once the foundation of the moral law and the explanation of our moral intuitions and perceptions.

So long as men remain men, the ethical rules by which they ought to live, and by which alone they can live rationally and successfully, will remain what they have been from the dawn of human creation. A changing world does not mean a changing ethics.

Ethics in a Changing World

By

PAUL J. TILLICH, D.D., Ph.D.*

"Changing world" in the title of my paper does not mean the general change implied in everything which exists; neither does it mean the continuous change connected more fundamentally with history than with nature; but it points to the fact that we are living in a historical period, characterized by a radical and revolutionary transformation of one historical era into another one. Nobody can doubt this fact seriously, and nobody who has even a minimum of historical judgment would do so after what has occurred during the last few months. We are in the midst of a world revolution, concerning every section of human existence, forcing upon us a new interpretation of life and the world. What about ethics in this connection? Does it represent a realm above change? Is it super-historical in its foundation, its values and its commands? Or does it follow the stream of historical becoming, and will it be transformed as rapidly as the other realms of life are transformed in our days? If the latter be the case which authority, which power of shaping human life is left to it? Can the unconditional claim with which every moral demand imposes itself on human conscience be maintained if the contents of the demand are different in every period of history? But if the former be the case, if ethics constitutes a realm above history, immovable and unconcerned by historical change, how can it influence man, living in history and transformed by history? Would it not remain a strange body within the context of human experience, separated from it in untouchable remoteness, subject perhaps to awe but without actual influence on the life process? In order to answer these questions and to refer them to our present situation I intend to deal first with some solutions appearing in the history of human thought which are still of a tremendous actual importance; second, I want to give my own

* Professor of Philosophical Theology, Union Theological Seminary.

solution; and third, I will try to apply this solution to the
present world situation by giving some practical examples.

I

There are three great types of life and thought representing
three different solutions of the problem of ethics in historical
change: First, the static-supra-naturalistic solution, represented
by the Roman Catholic Church and expressed in the ethics of
Thomas Aquinas. Second, the dynamic-naturalistic solution,
represented by the National Socialist movement and expressed
in the ethics of the philosophers of life. Third, the progressive-
rationalistic solution, represented by bourgeois democracy and
expressed in the ethics of the philosophers of reason. The static-
supra-naturalistic solution maintains, strongly and with a tremendous psychological power, the eternal and immovable character of the ethical norms and commands. Philosophy and
theology coöperate in this direction. The world is conceived
as a system of eternal structures, preformed in the divine mind,
which are substance and essence of everything, and establish
the norms and laws for man's personal and social practice.
Philosophy discovers these structures and laws, revelation confirms and amends them. And revelation adds some of its own:
superstructures, new and higher laws but equally eternal and
immovable. Both the natural and supra-natural structures together form a hierarchy of powers and values which control
nature and are supposed to control human activities. The
Church, itself a hierarchical system, teaches this system, edu-
cates for it, fights for its political realization, defends it against
new systems. But in doing so the Church cannot disregard the
actual situation and the historical changes. The Church must
adapt its ethical system to new problems and new demands. The
Catholic Church was able to do so in an admirable way for
centuries, and the living authority of the Pope is still a marvel-
ous instrument for achieving adaptations without losing its immovable basis. Nevertheless it is obvious that the Catholic
Church did not fully succeed in dealing with the bourgeois era,
its presuppositions and demands. Protestantism and Enlightenment created new systems of ethics besides, and against the
supposedly eternal system of the medieval Church. And when
the Church tried to go with the stream of the rising bourgeoisie,

as for instance in the moral preachings of seventeenth- and eighteenth-century Jesuitism and in the teachings of nineteenth-century Modernism, it either lost its seriousness and authority or it gave the bad impression of a fight of retreat in which every position is defended as long as possible and then surrendered. And the important utterances of the Holy See during the nineteenth century to the social and political problems presuppose in order to be applicable the unbroken unity and authority of the Christian Church which no longer exists. Therefore they did not influence at all the spirit of modern ethics and the road of bourgeois society. The price paid by the static-supra-naturalistic answer to our question was the loss of a determining influence on the changing world of the last centuries.

The opposite solution, represented by National Socialism, was prepared in two main ways, by the continental philosophy of life and by Anglo-American Positivism and Pragmatism, the latter being only a different form of the philosophy of life. National Socialism has used and abused the philosophical motives of the continental philosophy of life, especially of Nietzsche, Pareto, and Sorel. Philosophy must express life in its changing forms and trends. Truth, according to Nietzsche, is that lie which is useful for a special genus of beings. Values are produced and withdrawn in the dynamic process of life, biologically spoken by the strongest kind of living beings, sociologically spoken by the new élite, politically spoken by the eruptive violence of a revolutionary group. Change, being the main character of life, is also the main character of ethics. There are no independent norms above life, no criteria by which power could be judged, no standards for a good life. Good life is strong life or violent life or the life of a ruling aristocracy or the life of a conquering race. This implies that the individual, instead of being guided by the ethical norms which are manifest in his conscience, is obliged to merge his conscience into the group conscience. He must coördinate his standards with the group standards as represented by the leaders of the group. The dynamic-naturalistic type of answering the question of ethics in a changing world has a primitive-tribal character. It is, historically speaking, at the same time the most recent and the most ancient of all solutions of the ethical problem.

I have mentioned Anglo-Saxon Positivism and Pragmatism

in this connection, and it is perhaps an important task of this paper to make it clear that Pragmatism and philosophy of life belong to the same type of ethical dynamism. Pragmatism, in speaking of experience, surrenders the criteria of truth and the good no less than does the philosophy of life. There are no norms above the dynamic process of experience, namely, experienced life. The question, which kind of life creates ethical experience and which are the standards of a true ethical experience, is not answered and cannot be answered within the context of pragmatic thought. Therefore the Pragmatists and Positivists take their refuge to an ethical instinct which is supposed to lead to an ethical common sense. This refuge is secure as long as there is a society with a strong common belief and conventional morals, maintained by the leading groups of society. So it was in the acme of the bourgeois development, for instance, the Victorian era. But it did not work any more when the harmony of a satisfied society slowly disappeared and dissatisfied groups, masses, and nations asked for a new order of life. The ethical instinct of those groups was much different from the ethical instincts of the victorious Victorian bourgeoisie, and the refuge to ethical instinct and to common sense became ineffective. Pragmatism and Positivism were unable to face this threat because in their basic ideas they agree with the principles of the philosophy of life. The intellectual defense of the Anglo-Saxon civilization against the Fascist ideologies is extremely weak. Common sense, philosophy, and Pragmatism are not able to provide criteria against the dynamic irrationalism of the new movements, and they are not able to awaken the moral power of resistance which is needed for the maintenance of the humanistic values, embodied in the "Western" and Anglo-Saxon civilization. It is not Positivism and Pragmatism but the remnants of the rationalistic-progressive solution of the ethical problem on which the future of that civilization is based. This solution is the most natural one for an undisturbed bourgeois thought and is still deeply rooted in the subconscious of our contemporary philosophers as well as of men of practice. There are, according to this point of view, some eternal principles, the natural law of morals—but without the supra-natural sanction it obtains in the Catholic system. These principles, as embodied in the Bill of Rights, are like stars which always remain far remote from every human realization, but which like stars show the direction in which mankind must go. Once discovered, they cannot disappear any more, although their theoretical and practical realization is always in a process towards a higher perfection. In this way they are adaptable to every human situation. Is this the solution of the problem of ethics in a changing world? In some ways it is, in some ways not. It indicates the direction in which the solution must be sought. There must be something immovable in the ethical principle, the criterion and standard of all ethical change. And there must be a power of change in the ethical principle; and both must be united. But the rational-progressive solution is far from reaching this unity. It establishes some principles, as freedom and equality, in the name of the absolute natural law, to be found in nature and human reason at any time, in any place. Mankind is supposed to realize these principles, theoretically and practically, in a process of approximation. It is the same natural law, the same principles which always are more or less known, more or less received in reality. "More or less" points to a quantitative difference, but not to a qualitative change, not to new creations in the ethical realm. Ethics in a changing world changes only quantitatively, namely, as far as progress or regression with respect to their realization is concerned. More or less freedom, more or less equality is admitted, but not a new freedom or a new equality. The principles on which the progressive-rationalistic solution is based represent a special pattern, a special type of freedom and equality, that of the later ancient or that of the modern bourgeois period. They do not represent principles large enough to embrace all periods and creative enough to bring new embodiments of themselves. They are not eternal enough to be ultimate principles, and not temporal enough to fit a changing world. Therefore, as the Catholic system was not able to adapt itself seriously to the modern period of bourgeois growth, so the bourgeois-progressive rationalism was not able to face the breakdown of the bourgeois world. Supra-natural and rational absolutism in ethics, both proved to be unable to adapt themselves to a fundamental change of the historical situation.

II

Is there a possible solution beyond the alternative of an absolutism which breaks down in every radical change of history, and a relativism which makes the change itself the ultimate

principle? I think it is, and I think it is implied in the basis of
Christian ethics, namely in the principle of love in the sense of
the Greek word *agape*. This is not said in an apologetic interest
for Christianity, but it is said under the urge of the actual problem in our present world situation. Love, *agape,* offers a principle of ethics which maintains an eternal, unchangeable
element, but makes its realization dependent on continuous
acts of a creative intuition. Love is above law, also above the
natural law in Stoicism and the supra-natural law in Catholicism. You *can* express it as a law, you can say as Jesus and the
apostles did: "You shall love"; but in doing so you know that
this is a paradoxical way of speaking, indicating that the ultimate principle of ethics, which on the one hand is an incondi-
tioned command, on the other hand is the power breaking
through all commands. And just this ambiguous character of
love enables it to be the solution of the question of ethics in a
changing world. If you look at the principles of natural law as
embodied in the Bill of Rights you will find that taken as the
concrete embodiments of the principle of love in a special situation they are great and true and powerful; they represent love
by establishing freedom and equal rights against willfulness and
suppression and against the destruction of the dignity of human
beings. But taken as eternal laws and applied legalistically to
different situations, for instance, the early middle ages or the
decay and transformation of economic capitalism, these principles became bad ideologies, used for the maintenance of
decaying institutions and powers. This is the reason for the
extremely profound struggle of Paul and Luther against the
"Law" and for their insistence on the mortifying consequences
of the law and the vivifying power of love. *Love alone can transform itself according to the concrete demands of every individual and social situation without losing its eternity and dignity
and unconditioned validity.* Love can adapt itself to every phase
of a changing world. I like to introduce at this place another
Greek word, namely *kairos*, the right time. This word, used in
common Greek, has received an emphatic meaning in the
language of the New Testament, designating the fulfillment
of time in the appearance of the Christ. It has been reinter-
preted by German Religious Socialism in the sense of a special
gift and a special task breaking from internity into history at
a special time. *Kairos* in this sense is the historical moment in

which something new, eternally important, manifests itself in temporal forms, in the potentialities and tasks of a special period. It is the power of the prophetic spirit in all periods of history to pronounce the coming of such a *kairos*, to discover its meaning, to express the criticism of what is given and the hope for what is to come. All great changes in history are accompanied by a strong consciousness of a *kairos* at hand. Therefore ethics in a changing world must be understood as ethics of the *kairos*. The solution of the question for ethics in a changing world is ethics determined by the *kairos*; but only love is able to appear in every *kairos*. Law is not able because law is the attempt to impose something which belonged to a special time on all times. An ideal which has appeared at the right time and is valid for this time is considered to be the ideal for history as a whole, as that form of life in which history shall find its end. The outcome of this attitude necessarily is disillusionment and the rise of ethical libertinism and relativism. This is the point in which the dynamic-naturalistic solution in spite of its destructive consequences was right and still is right against Catholic and bourgeois ethics. Or, the same idea expressed in terms of Church history: This is the point in which Luther is right against Thomas and Calvin. Love realizing itself from *kairos* to *kairos* creates ethics which is beyond the alternative of absolute and relative ethics.

III

This solution now may be explained and made more concrete by some examples.

First I want to deal with the idea of equality, one of the foundations of rational-progressive ethics. In the light of the principle of love and in the perspective of the idea of *kairos* the following statements can be made: Love implies equality in some respect. He who loves and he who is loved are equal for each other as far as they are worthy of love the one for the other. But nothing else than just this principle of equality is implied—essentially implied—in love. Everything else is historical embodiment of that principle in different situations with love and the distortion of love at the same time. Looking at a Greek city-state we discover that there is a political equality between the individuals within a special group and, to a certain extent, between all those who are free; but there is an absolute inequality between the free and the slaves. Love is not manifest as *the* principle, but since it potentially is the principle, it is effective even in the religion and culture of Apollo and Dionysos. It is effective in the kind of equality the city-state gives to those who belong to it, excluding slaves and barbarians. Love is effective even in this restricted equality, but a restricted, distorted love, love in the boundaries of national eros and political law. The central *kairos* in which love has become manifest as what it really is had not yet appeared. And it had not appeared either, when Stoicism in the period of the universal Roman Empire extended equality to all human beings, men and women, children and slaves. In these ideas the principle of love breaks through the limitations of national eros and law, but it does so, not as love, but as universal law without eros. The stoic equality is universal but cool and abstract, without the warmth and the erotic element of the limited equality in the city-state. At its best it is participation in Roman citizenship and in the possibility of becoming a wise man. In the Christian event love has become manifest in its universality, but at the same time in its concreteness: The "neighbor" is the immediate object of love, and everybody can become "neighbor." All inequalities between man are overcome as far as they are potential children of God. But this did not lead Christianity to the stoic idea of equality. Not even the inequality between lord and slave was attacked except in the realm of faith and love. Later not the totalitarian but the hierarchical principle was supported by the Christian Church according to the late ancient and medieval situation. The social and psychological inequalities of the feudal order did not seem to contradict the element of equality implied in the principle of love. On the contrary, the mutual interdependence of all the degrees of the hierarchy, the solidarity of all the members of a medieval city and the patriarchalistic care of the feudal lords for their "people" were considered as the highest form of equality, demanded by the principle of love. In bourgeois liberalism equality was again interpreted in terms of the general natural law, the law of reason and humanity. Equality became equality before the law and the demand for equal economic chances. This was in accordance with the principle of love over against the tyranny and injustice into which the older system had developed. But in the measure in which the equal chance of everybody became a mere ideology to cover the exclusive chance for a few, the liberal idea of equality became a contradiction of love. A new idea of equality has risen, the meaning of which is equal security of everyone, even if much political equality must be sacrificed. One must not condemn the collectivistic and authoritarian forms of equality because they are the negation of its liberal and democratic forms. Love may demand this transformation in our *kairos*. A new creative realization of the element of equality as implied in the principle of love may be brought about in our period. It will be good as far as it is in better accordance with the demands of love in our special situation than the liberal and feudal forms were. It will be bad as far as it is a distortion and contradiction of love as it actually is. For love is eternal although it creates something new in each *kairos*.

I could refer to many more ethical problems in order to show their double dependence, on the principle of love on the one hand, on the changing *kairos* on the other hand. For instance, I could point to the valuation of work and activism in the different periods of history and their relation to leisure and meditation. It is obvious that the coming collectivism will reduce the emphasis on work and activism considerably by restraining the principle of competition. As the struggle against some forms of feudal and ecclesiastical leisure and meditative life was a demand of love in the period of the decaying middle ages, and in the moment in which mankind started its control over nature and its general rise to a higher standard of technical civilization, so it is now a demand of love and of our *kairos* that leisure and meditation return on the basis of a new collectivistic structure of society over against a self-destructive adoration of work and activism.

Another example is the problem of asceticism and worldliness, of self-control and self-expression, of discipline and creativity in their relation to each other. Both sides follow from the principle of love. The negation of the first would prevent the self-surrender implied in love, the negation of the second would destroy any subject worth being loved. It depends on the *kairos*, which of these sides, in which form, and in which balance with the other side, is emphasized. For our present situation neither the supra-natural asceticism of the Catholic system, nor the

rational self-control of bourgeois society, nor the naturalistic
war- and state-discipline of Fascism can give the solution. And
the same is true of feudal eroticism, of bourgeois aestheticism,
and of Fascist adoration of vitality; another solution is demanded by love and by our *kairos*. Some elements of the solution are provided by psychoanalysis, although mere psycho-
therapeutic psychology is not able to create by itself a new
system of ethics. Other elements of the solution are brought
upon by the rediscovery of the classical meaning of *eros* and
by the different attempts to refer it to *agape*. The educational
movements and the criticism of the bourgeois ideal of family
have contributed a great deal. But everything is in motion, and
the criterion of the final solution is the measure in which *eros*
on the one hand, and self-control on the other hand, are shaped
by love.

A final question must be answered. If love is the principle
of ethics and *kairos* the way of its embodiment in concrete
contents, how can a permanent uncertainty, a continuous criticism, destroying the seriousness of the ethical demand, be
avoided? Is not law and are not institutions necessary in order
to maintain the actual ethical process? Indeed, law and institutions are demanded. They are demanded by love itself. For
the individual, every individual, even the most creative, needs
given structures which embody the experience and wisdom of
the past, which liberate him from the necessity of innumerable
decisions of its own, which show him a meaningful way of acting in most cases. In this point Catholicism was superior in
love both to Protestantism and Liberalism; and this is the reason why the younger generation in many countries eagerly
demand laws and institutions able to relieve them from the
unbearable burden of continuous ultimate decisions of their
own. No ethics ever can become an actual power without laws
and institutions. Luther in his great emphasis on the creativity
of love forgot this need. This is one of the reasons why the
moral education of the German masses is less thorough than
that in the Calvinistic countries. On the other hand, there is
more readiness for a *kairos* in Germany than in the highly educated and shaped western nations. Love demands laws and
institutions, but love is always able to break through them in
a new *kairos* and to create new laws and new systems of ethics.

I did not mention the word "justice." It has become misleading in the present discussion because it is generally understood in the sense of the abstract natural law of Stoicism and Rationalism. As such it is either empty or the concrete law of a special period, and without universal validity. If justice is taken concretely it means the laws and institutions in which love is embodied in a special situation. The Platonic ideal of justice was the concrete harmony of the city-state, in Israel justice was the pious obedience to the commands of God, in medieval feudalism the forms of mutual responsibility of all degrees of the hierarchy to each other; in liberalism the laws abolishing formal privileges and introducing legal equality. In the coming collectivism justice will be the system of laws and forms by which a sufficient security of the whole and of all members will be maintained and developed. From this it follows that justice is the secondary and derived principle, while love, actualized from *kairos* to *kairos*, is the creative and basic principle.

I gave no definition of love. This is impossible because there is no higher principle by which it could be defined. It is life itself in its actual unity. The forms and structures in which love embodies itself are the forms and structures in which life is possible, in which life overcomes its self-destructive forces. And this is the meaning of ethics: to express the ways in which love embodies itself and life is maintained and saved.

The Place of Religion in Higher Education

By

ROBERT L. CALHOUN, Ph.D.*

WITH civilization cracking, why trouble ourselves just now about higher education? Merely because we ourselves are engaged in it? No. Because without the things it stands for, there is no civilization worth the name. Civilized living is possible only for people at once disciplined and free. Such people are naturally not shut up in universities. There are doubtless more of them outside than inside our circles of higher education, with all their graduates and former students included. We have no monopoly of civilized living. But it remains true that the primary aim of unregimented colleges and universities is to help produce disciplined, free persons equipped to live in the complex, high-speed world of today. To this end they need religion, and religion needs them—or at least the things they stand for: trained intelligence, free inquiry, a critical temper, a clear-headed world outlook.

Complete education must provide at least three sorts of equipment for life: specialized skills, specialized knowledge of many sorts, and a perspective or unifying frame through which the details become a systematic whole.

The skills we need are work- and play-habits, practical ways of getting things done with precision and dispatch. Some are manual skills, some verbal. An educated person needs both. Some, again, are instrumental or utilitarian work-habits that are needed mainly to produce ulterior results, while others are expressive skills employed mainly for the immediate satisfaction of the activity itself. We learn to drive nails, cook, spell, run a typewriter, add and subtract, not for immediate pleasure but to provide ourselves with houses, meals, books, and income. We learn to dance, to sing, or to talk mainly for the joy of expressing our feelings and thoughts effectively. In either case,

* Professor of Historical Theology and Fellow of Saybrook College, Yale University.

a suitable education must provide the equipment for what we want to do.

It must provide also many varieties of special knowledge, both technical and cultural. These terms are neither exact nor fixed in meaning. What is technical knowledge for one person, needed to guide him in his work, may be cultural or humanizing knowledge without specific technical value for another. A surgeon has to know human anatomy, an engineer structural steel, a farmer soils and seeds. For each, technical knowledge in his own field is indispensable. If, on the other hand, the doctor knows also something of literature, the engineer a little biology, the farmer a bit of history, such knowledge will probably not make these men more expert workmen. It will almost surely make them better neighbors, citizens, human beings. This is cultural knowledge. Without it, higher education would produce efficient technicians equipped to make a living and to do useful work. It would not be adapted to help them understand their places in the natural world and the human struggle, and so to see what value their work has in relation to what others are doing and have done.

In principle, all these skills and special segments of knowledge are interrelated, but in practice they tend to become disconnected. An educated person therefore requires, besides these, a unifying or integrating frame to insure that the details shall be organized into a life with unity and direction. Our concern here is mainly with this third major factor in education, which must have two sides: an inclusive theoretic outlook or point of view from which the world and oneself can be understood after a fashion, and a no less inclusive practical dynamic or loyalty by which all that one is, thinks, and does may be vitalized and directed. The one side is intellectual perspective or philosophy, the other is religious devotion. Each needs the other, and higher education must make room for both. Without them its work is patchwork, not the making of unified persons, fit to bear civilization.

On its theoretic side, the perspective we need can be provided by the intellectual enterprise itself. That enterprise is not likely to be undervalued by any who read these words. Its contributions to civilized living are so obvious we take them for granted. It makes, first, for liberation. Specific technical knowledge—physical, medical, psychological—has freed us from many of the disabilities and fears that hamper untutored folk. We have our own superstitions, of course, but at least many that dogged our ancestors no longer trouble us. Our specific and tested knowledge applied through suitable technological procedures has made possible new modes of action, prediction, and control of our environment. It gives promise also of better understanding and control of ourselves; though it must be said that specific knowledge by itself is not likely ever to enable us to cope fully with the problems of evaluation and decision involved in personal growth. More than information, more even than philosophy, is needed for these tasks.

Liberation comes also through cultural understanding, and the development of an inclusive outlook, a personal world-view. Naturally no one can include in his perspective more than a small portion of reality. But the habit of trying to see one's problems, neighbors, interests in a wide context has its own value for human freedom. A persistent sense of the magnitude of the human panorama and some reasonable understanding of it brings release from provincialisms of time and place, and from at least some of the constricting prejudices that go with them. One who thinks in terms of the development of American life from the conquistadores to the New Deal is less likely to be fooled by party slogans than his neighbor who thinks only from one election to another, or who is aware only of the interests of his own business or his own part of the country. One who tries to think in terms of world history can see even American life as contributing to a larger whole; and a sense of geologic time is an excellent corrective to over-hasty optimism or pessimism about mankind.

A critical temper of mind, finally, should be one of the most distinctive results of serious intellectual activity. Not the sceptical temper, that believes nothing, and still less the cynical temper that believes only the worst. A critical mind is one that persists in asking relevant questions and demanding relevant answers. It is not to be put off with emphatic generalities, nor hocus-pocus bearing an authoritative stamp; though an honest acknowledgment of ignorance is always acceptable to a critical intelligence. Such a mind is quite ready to give hearty assent and whole-souled effort when fairly convinced, even where conclusive proof cannot be had. It is one mark of critical acumen to recognize that practical decisions often cannot wait on cogent proof, and that scepticism is not really a live alternative to personal commitment. But though commitments cannot be avoided, they can be guided, tested, and suitably proportioned to the realities that call them forth. A trained mind is freed from naïve bondage to any partial schemes of living, old or new. Knowledge thus far *is* power, and truth does make men free.

No less truly, high-grade intellectual work makes for discipline of very basic kinds—the kinds that grow within growing persons, not the kinds that are put on like plaster casts and stop growth. There is intrinsic discipline in the very doing of intellectual work: methods to be mastered, accumulated knowledge to be learned and tested. We are not raising here the threadbare question of "formal discipline" as a special virtue of certain studies, especially the ones that young learners find the more tiresome. The point here is not that learning irregular Latin verbs or ways to factor quadratic equations has moral value in general, nor even that it develops intellectual powers of some generalized sort. The point is simply that in becoming expert in any area of knowledge and inquiry, one comes to be a person disciplined by the requirements of that specific area, a trained worker who knows in at least one field the difference between random and directed effort.

Besides this, there is discipline of a more purely social sort that comes through association with experienced workers in a chosen vocation. The group habits of doctors, lawyers, scientists, lay hold on their younger associates and develop in them the *savoir faire* of trained professional men and women. This is partly a knowledge of professional etiquette and the unwritten codes of groups that have a long tradition and strong group consciousness. To become a junior member of such a company is to assume responsibilities not unlike those of a medieval guild or monastic order. Names for the status of apprenticeship or novitiate change, but the realities endure. The young lawyer or engineer learns the ways of a calling largely by contact with its experienced practitioners who are his teachers and elder colleagues. Knowledge so acquired is discipline, and such tempering is no less vital than freedom. Intellectual life at its best provides both.

Yet the intellectual enterprise even at its best has limitations, and these are the more evident in our far from perfect versions of that enterprise. One is a tendency to confusing diversity. The immense bulk of what is now known about men and the world makes necessary a minute subdivision of labor in the quest for more knowledge. No single worker can know thoroughly more than a tiny corner of the whole field of knowledge today. Scientists and scholars necessarily become specialists, and students are likely to find the college and university courses based on their work tending to present human knowledge in fragments, not as a living whole. Any attempt to remedy this admittedly bad situation by trying to eliminate or to regiment the specialists, even the more narrowly technical of them, who are engaged in genuine inquiry, would be an attempt to turn back the clock. Whatever integration of knowledge is still possible must come through collaboration of specialists and sagacious plain people intent on fitting their own ideas together and getting a sense of life as a whole. Such collaboration is difficult, and such integration of thought in the minds of educated laymen is all too rare. Philosophers should be able to offer especially valuable help toward it, when they have not themselves become super-specialists and lost sight of the need for continuous integration, even while methods are still imperfect and data incomplete—as they always will be. Until this need is more steadily recognized and effectively met, our intellectual advances will continue to make for confusion as well as for liberation and special discipline.

More than that, the pure intellectual impulse to seek knowledge as such is a fragile disposition, late in development and difficult to maintain. Far more than the cruder vital drives— hunger and the like—that keep men alive as animals, this distinctively human impulse is liable to damage by emotional upheavals. It is not simply the falsehoods of propaganda ministries that make truth proverbially the first casualty in war time. Under the stress of strong fear or anger, from which not even scientists and scholars are immune, it may become almost impossible to tell the truth or to recognize it. And one who tries especially hard to avoid such emotional involvement and distortion may succeed at the cost of his normal human responsiveness. He becomes then an onlooker at the human scene, the victim of an "academic" detachment grown into an obsession. Such men are the sceptical positivists of all times and cultures, who recognize so clearly and dread so acutely the precariousness of intellectual objectivity that they deliberately sacrifice to it other habits no less distinctively human and no less essential to humane living. Thinking machines, no matter how accurate, are not men. To produce them in large numbers would be little to the credit of a civilized university. For humane civilization needs loyalties quite as much as it needs ideas.

Against these various dangers of the intellectual life there is no panacea, but there is a powerful antidote, once more prevalent in higher education than it has been recently. Religion of the right sort can provide a dynamic unity of experience more inclusive even than the theoretic unity of a metaphysics, and vigorous enough to withstand even the disrupting forces of anger and fear. It can provide, moreover, a kind of motivation that will forestall any tendency to passive onlooking, and at the same time will tend strongly to keep the active participation of its devotees above narrow partisanships or selfish opportunism. Religion of the right sort; not lip-religion or ceremonies out of touch with everyday practice, nor yet tribal fanaticism of either the old or the newer types.

In sharp contrast to the perfunctory thing sometimes called by the same name, essential religion is dynamic as few other forces in human life can be. It is man's response to a Presence in his world so overwhelming to him that he cannot disregard, escape, or control it. This is for him "the Holy," his God. The reality that affects a particular man or people in this way may have any of a wide variety of characters. It may be a natural object, a magnified human person, a nation-state or people, mankind, the universe as we know it, or a God beyond all these. In any event, if it provokes a genuine religious response, it has for the one who worships it the status of a reality that transcends his own powers, is inaccessible and uncontrollable by his efforts, making claims upon him that he cannot ignore if he would. In worship he stands in awe before it, finds himself powerfully united to it, and gives to it his supreme loyalty, without bargaining or reservation. Such reality, whether it be a nature-deity, a deified monarch or Führer, an exalted nation, class, or people, or a transcendent God of justice and love, exerts compulsive power upon the lives of worshipers, exacting of them sacrificial loyalty, and often breaking through the established patterns of their thought and lives in unpredictable ways. Religious devotees are men and women in the grip of tremendous emotional powers that shape and direct their living.

The response of such men and women is religious faith: commitment without reservation to the God adored, and to his demands. In general terms, this means a reorientation of the whole life of the worshiper, which becomes so pervaded by the inclusive loyalty to his God that lesser loyalties are rejected or absorbed, and his life unified toward one supreme goal: the Kingdom of God, in whatever terms it be conceived. This reorientation is not a simple matter of choice, still less of verbal inference. It takes place below the surface of thought and conscious feeling. The very springs of conduct and of consciousness are reshaped by it. But this hidden reordering (called in the Christian tradition by such names as regeneration, redemption, divine calling—God's grace awakening man's faith) shows itself in the conscious life of the devotee, the man of faith who has heard the call of his God and is answering with all his heart and strength. Such men and women become unmanageable by the ordinary tools of persuasion or force. Something of the uncontrollability of the divine Reality reappears in them, and they become shock troops, rebels, or martyrs of the sort that secular powers have always found hardest to handle, because they are no longer moved mainly by self-interest. Once they have said to God (or to the state or the Führer), "Not my will, but thine be done," they have ceased to be ordinary egos, drawn this way and that by the shifting objects of their personal desires. They have become bondservants of their God, who find in his service a new kind of self-realization that men can neither give nor take away.

But the very strength of religion thus understood involves perils too obvious and familiar to need much discussion here. All the more since we have spread before our eyes, in every morning and evening paper, the record of fierce religions of our own day gone wrong. Living religion almost inevitably exalts the emotional and impulsive side of human living, and tends to be impatient of thought, especially critical thought. Deliberation is likely to seem temporizing, and criticism sheer treason, giving aid and comfort to the enemy. It is a rare and difficult religion that enjoins love for one's enemies, who tend easily to become identified in the devotee's mind as God's enemies, who should be shouted down or stamped out, not coddled or "understood." Critical thinking, dispassionate inquiry, equitable judication are hard to reconcile with the headlong, all-or-none tendency of authentic religious devotion.

In its more popular forms, moreover, such religion (or quasi-religion) tends to fixate its terrible loyalties on natural or cultural objects of worship—on power as such, or on a hero or a deified state or people. So it loses sight of the transcendent element in essential religion that drives men who are aware of its meaning to look beyond every hero and every social order to a God who is more than these. Fanaticism and idolatry are the bane of crude, powerful religion, as escapism is the bane of academic intellectual life. And flight into chaos can be quite as disastrous as any "flight from chaos" into an isolationist tower.

Religion needs the closest association with intellectual discipline and liberating insight, if its driving force is to make for humane life. It needs the repeated test of comparison with the ranges of known fact, to keep its drives relevant to the actual requirements of human well-being in the actual world. It needs the critical temper of fine-edged minds constantly at work to keep its perspective clear, to make impossible its mistaking some partial, relative, created thing, human or inhuman, for the transcendent Reality that alone deserves adoration. This is why religion needs for its own good health a place in the enterprise of higher education, where the intellectual life is especially cherished.

Not all religion, by a great deal, can stand that sort of association. The cruder tribalisms of our time are crushing free intellectual life, and impressing the minds of their scientists and scholars into the service of gods that cannot bear the light of critical inquiry. Christianity, for all the spottedness of its record in relation to such inqury, shines by contrast with these newly god-intoxicated secularisms. They by their very nature are constrained to shun thoroughgoing inquiry, since they seek to maintain as authoritative mythical truth various doctrines—the master race, the classless Utopia, the decadence of peace-loving peoples—that are demonstrably contrary to known or probable facts. Their myths depend for plausibility on the elevation of partial realities and relative values into absolutes. Rectification of this perspective, such as free critical inquiry would bring about, must destroy the very basis of any idolatrous, creature-worshiping religion. On the contrary, a religion whose only God is the God of all truth, justice, and mercy who is beyond every race and class, the one God of nature and all mankind, can only gain through such rectification. Idolatry is of the essence of secularistic religions. It is a perversion of Christianity, which is the better for critical purging that continually works against such perversion.

High religion, in short, and intellectual enterprise belong together. Each gains from close association with the other. The two in conjunction, but neither one by itself, can move with hope toward more effective conquest of the chaos that again and again threatens to engulf human living. That way lies whatever chance we may have for a more humane world.

The Place of Religion in Higher Education

By

CHARLES W. GILKEY, D.D.*

DURING a recent term of service as visiting preacher at Harvard, I asked one of the younger assistants there what changes he had noted in the attitude toward religion of the present student generation as compared with their predecessors. His well-remembered reply will indicate not only the approach but the central thesis of this paper. "Five years ago," he said, "our best men here were saying with a shrug of their shoulders, when you asked them about religion: 'Religion? Nothing to it!' Today," he went on, "their successors are asking: 'Religion? What is there in it?' "

It happens that since I entered college as a freshman forty-one years ago, I have had practically continuous personal contacts with ten successive four-year generations of American college students, chiefly in the East and Middle West. The only considerable interruptions were a two-year period of study in the German and British universities before the Great War, and a later visit as Barrows Lecturer to the university centers of India. During the last thirty of these forty-one years, I have served as a minister of religion next door to the University of Chicago. For the last twelve years I have given all my time to the religious life and work of that university community, with frequent visits also to other campuses east and west, north and south—many of them for days at a time. Within the last year, for instance, I have served as visiting preacher at various private institutions from Harvard on the east to Stanford on the west; and I have spoken on religion at various state institutions from Oregon on the northwest to Florida on the southeast. This paper is chiefly concerned with and based upon these personal experiences and observations of present religious trends in American colleges and universities.

* Associate Dean of the Divinity School and Dean of the Chapel, University of Chicago.

It is my definite impression that there have been greater changes during the last five years in the attitude of the present student generation toward religion, as compared with its immediate predecessor, than during any other similar period in the forty years of my own observation.

I should not for a moment think of describing these changes as "a revival of religion." That familiar phrase has too precise and technical a significance in American religious history to permit its application with any accuracy to the present religious attitudes of American students. The highly organized social pressure, the psychological absorption, the emotional stress and strain of the traditional religious revival, are on most American campuses conspicuous these days chiefly by their absence: indeed, the present student generation is far less familiar with these particular religious phenomena than were its predecessors. The changes I have in mind are far more inconspicuous, and therefore much more easily overlooked or misinterpreted. Their nature and direction are clearly reflected in the Harvard comment already quoted. There is much less disposition today than yesterday to dismiss religion with the dogmatic finality or sophisticated indifference that so confidently said, "Religion? Nothing to it!" There is much more readiness to consider its validity and also its challenge, with a sensitiveness and responsiveness that sometimes include wistfulness as well. "Religion? What is there in it?"

Nor do I mean to suggest that these changes are everywhere in evidence. It is almost as dangerous to generalize about any generation as Burke said it was to indict an entire nation. I have myself visited more than one campus during recent years where those in the best position to judge report little or no change in the religious situation during the last five years. I have been reminded, in this as in other contemporary connections, of a situation that often perplexes those of us who summer on the Maine coast, when the tide is pretty well out. Ominous rocks and far-reaching flats are so plainly in evidence, and the water-line seems to be so nearly where it was an hour or two ago, that it is easy to jump to the conclusion that little if anything has changed in the interval. But a closer look out into the channel shows that the buoys have swung over and are pointing in a new direction, and on the shelving bits of beach between the huge masses of rocks in the foreground the bubbles are brimming and the ripples rising. The tide has turned.

The purpose of this paper is to look for such significant signs of change in places that may at first sight seem inconspicuous; then, if these are found, to seek the causes that are producing them; and finally, to ask what any such changes and causes may indicate as to the place of religion in the higher education of the next generation. It will be evident at once that this paper does not approach its subject by way of a particular philosophy of either education or religion, the logical consequences of which the paper then proceeds to expound or elaborate; nor yet is it primarily a survey of present religious policies and organizational set-ups, either official or voluntary, in our American colleges and universities. It is rather a report of personal observation and experience; and if there is distortion or lack of perspective in its reporting, that will come either from the limitations of my experience, or from my own misinterpretation of it. Professors Niebuhr and Calhoun have spoken to us this morning as distinguished theologians and experienced educators can and should. My contribution is not so much that of an educator, a theologian, or even an administrator, as it is that of a neighbor and friend of successive student generations, whose recent years have been spent in trying to work out with them, both in practice and in theory, an interrelation between religion and education which will best prepare them for life in the changing and critical days in which their lot is cast.

I

What signs are there then of a changed or changing attitude toward religion on the part of the present student generation? In a recent conversation with Rufus Jones, who is surely a dean among all American college preachers and is happily not yet emeritus, he remarked that these were the best days he had ever seen for preaching to students, because so many of them come out to chapel services, and come in such a questing and responsive mood. That must have been the experience of many much less magnetic college preachers than Dr. Jones: certainly it has been my own. So I mention first—though its significance is perhaps not so great as this place of emphasis would seem to imply—what seems to be a widespread trend toward increased student attendance at chapel services where these are entirely voluntary, and provide therefore an unbiased barometer of student interest. Any form of compulsory chapel attendance, any recent controversy about it, or any recent change in institutional policy at this point, introduces elements that complicate and confuse the situation too much to make chapel attendance significant for our purposes today. But where attendance has been voluntary for a considerable period, I believe that such a trend is widely evident.

In my own student days at Harvard forty years ago, for instance, it used to be notorious, as it was likewise when I first knew the University of Chicago thirty years ago, that neighbors and visitors in the community went to chapel, but hardly any students. I have preached at Harvard at least often enough in recent years not to rate in any sense as a curiosity or a magnet: but as an alumnus as well as a visiting preacher, I have been interested on my last two visits to find more students in Sunday chapel than I myself ever saw there before. When I asked the chapel janitor about this (and chapel janitors usually know what is going on), he told me that the total attendance at daily chapel up to that date (in March) was two thousand above that to the same date the year before. I have preached at Cornell oftener in recent years than at Harvard—and never to so many students as in the last five years. I am told that this is the experience of most visiting preachers at both universities. Certainly it is our own experience at Chicago. We have kept careful record of our congregations at the Sunday morning service since the dedication of our University Chapel in 1928. The total attendance at that service—in conformity I suspect with church attendance all over the country—is slowly going down. But at the same time that the total is falling, the number of students in the congregation, in the unanimous opinion of student ushers, janitors, and frequent attendants, has been steadily and even more sharply going up, both relatively and absolutely. One of our most regular visiting preachers recently remarked that when he first came to our chapel, his hearers seemed to be mostly community folk and visitors: but now, he went on, this is a congregation of youth—as it ought to be.

Nor is this observation confined to private institutions whose tradition it is to maintain chapel services. President Elliott of

Purdue, concerned because so many students in that great state university had no contact with contemporary religious movements and leaders, inaugurated several years ago a series of university convocations for public worship, about six weeks apart on Sunday mornings, with representatives of the chief religious bodies, Jewish and Catholic as well as Protestant, invited by the university itself as speakers. On the two Sunday mornings when I have had the honor of such an invitation, my experience has been that of practically every visiting speaker; we have found Fowler Hall overcrowded with more than a thousand students and faculty—and many standing. Next year, I am told, these occasional Sunday convocations are to be moved to the Field House for more room.

But while voluntary chapel attendance may be in various institutions an initial sign of quickened religious interest, I am inclined to see even more significance in something much less obvious: the greater readiness of more students to identify themselves publicly with religion by personal participation in religious services. Ten years ago I should never have dreamed of asking undergraduates at the University of Chicago to take any part in our chapel services: to that sophisticated student generation, the thing simply wasn't done! For the last two or three years, however, the Scripture has been read every Sunday morning by a student; and so many students have volunteered for this, that we have held a regular training class with competent coaching, out of which the best readers are chosen. This may seem to outsiders a small matter: but those who know college campuses will understand the incredulity of many of our alumni; remembering only the attitude of their own contemporaries in these matters, they are inclined to say of our present student readers what the sceptic at the circus said when he saw the giraffe: "No, there *ain't* no such animal!"

Statistics from campus religious organizations and activities so often reflect factors that are largely local or temporary, that they hardly serve as clear evidence for our present purpose: but every now and then the most hardened statistical sceptic runs into surprises. With more of our own students now living and working at the University Settlement back of the Stock Yards than ever before in its forty-five-year history, I knew something of the readiness of this student generation to show its faith by its works. But I was not prepared for what I found when I went two years ago to the University of Virginia to give its annual lectures on religion, and was surprised, as one so often is these days in universities that are not supposed to be "long" on religion, by the attendance and response. When I asked a group of upperclassmen what changes they had noted in religious attitudes since they entered college, one senior, who I understand is now studying for the ministry, replied that he had been impressed by the increasing number of students who were going out every Sunday to conduct religious services in isolated mountain communities where otherwise there would be no public worship. When I asked how many such there would be on a typical Sunday, he referred me to the Episcopal rector who organized these deputations. The rector said that until he could get an assistant to handle this whole growing enterprise, sixty-eight to seventy students a week-end was all that he could manage—what with cars to arrange for as well as students, and all the work of his own large parish to carry meanwhile. It was the same outgoing sense of social and spiritual responsibility that I have been more recently impressed by in the summer camp for underprivileged boys supported and manned by the Student-Faculty Association at Princeton; and likewise by the less known but equally significant work done by the girls at Wesleyan College in Georgia for the underprivileged young women of their own city—especially its industrial workers.

Perhaps the most characteristic of these trends, however, just because it is least conspicuous to outsiders and "cometh not with observation," is the quickened interest in the discussion of religious questions, both between individuals and in informal groups. Of course "bull sessions" on religion, spontaneous more often than organized, have always been more frequent in dormitories and fraternity houses than outsiders guess; and they often reveal religious views quite different from those that are supposed to be prevalent among students. Theological as well as social and political conservatism, and strong ecclesiastical loyalties, turn up much oftener among both students and faculties than those realize who so often criticize our colleges as hotbeds of radicalism.

But while there has thus always been student interest in religious discussion, especially between divergent points of view, I suspect that the most revealing change of recent years has shown itself in this general area. Ten years ago, I was regularly told by our Chicago students when planning the programs for our informal Sunday evening discussion groups, that they were very much interested in social questions—but of course nobody was interested in religious problems any more! When our religious discussion group started four years ago, it was a very small beginning. During the last year or two we have had Sunday evening groups meeting in two or three faculty homes, usually two on the social issues about which students are as much concerned as ever, and one on religious questions. Time and again the attendance at the religious problems group has been larger than at the other two put together; and when these last two broke up for the evening, some of their most earnest souls would come over to the religious group, confident that after two hours of discussion they would find some heads still together in a corner around the faculty or visiting leader, still going strong. . . .

I do not mean to imply that a student discussion group is the last word in a campus religious program, or that it always finds answers to the questions it raises. As a matter of fact, it may spread doubts and difficulties about religion almost as often as it solves them. The frequent summary of students themselves, after long hours spent in ranging over the ancient and ultimate questions of human life and destiny, says simply, "We got nowhere." The spiritual pulse-beat of these discussion groups is rarely full and strong like that of the early Christians in their love-feasts, or the early Methodists in their class-meetings—or even like that of the modern Oxford Groupers. Whatever we may think of the theology or the sociology of the latter, there can be little doubt that in their emphasis on the small group of kindred spirits as the creative religious unit, they have recovered something that has been characteristic of Christianity in all its greatest epochs. For there is obviously a very important difference between sharing in a discussion of religious problems that perplex the participants, and sharing in a positive faith that is common to most if not all of the members of the group. But when that important distinction has been fully recognized, it is also true that Jesus promised his deepest religious disclosures to those who "ask . . . seek . . . knock." That familiar promise suggests that there are real religious possibilities in a student generation so many of whom have begun to ask with such earnestness, "Religion? What is there in it?"

The University Missions of the last two years have been at once an effect and a cause of this quickened student concern with religion. Launched by the general conviction of the major religious agencies at work among students, that the times were ripe for a united and aggressive approach to some twoscore strategic institutions during the last two years, these Christian Missions have brought to these campuses for a week teams of younger religious leaders, whose best work has frequently been done in group discussions in fraternity and sorority houses, dormitories, and classrooms, as well as in central faculty and student gatherings. The response of administrative officers and faculties has usually been as cordial as that of students; and where the coöperation and preparation of the local religious agencies has been thorough, the results have been proportionate. I shall long remember the days at North Dakota State College at Fargo, where the complete coöperation of faculty, students, the administration not least, and the local churches as well, focused the increasing attention of the entire campus on religion, for a week as memorable as any such that I can recall in scores of such undertakings across thirty years.

II

What now are some of the factors that, under varying local conditions and in different degrees, combine to produce these trends? Among these complicated causes, I should give substantial weight to the increasing religious illiteracy of American undergradutes. They are very often the children of parents who, for any one or more of a dozen reasons, have loosened such religious connections as they may have had before or just after these children were born, and have since given them little or no religious training at home. President Butler of Columbia has warned us that America is passing into a new Dark Ages in respect to the ignorance on the part of its rising generation of its two great classics, Shakespeare and the English Bible. If time permitted, I could convulse you with instances of this ignorance so far as the Bible is concerned. This cultural and spiritual illiteracy applies almost equally to the entire ethical and religious heritage of Christianity. It leaves them exposed, without the discriminating perspectives which the student of the history of all religions soon develops, to the contemporary "isms" that promise the modern man salvation—especially when these carry religious elements within their dogmatisms; and it equally leaves them exposed to the plausibilities of those current schools of theology and philosophy that find their finalities in the thinking of some authoritative past. As thoughtful students become aware of this insulation from their spiritual heritage, they often become more curious, and sometimes more wistful, about the religion of their fathers.

This curiosity is directly related to the *serious-mindedness* of a steadily increasing proportion of this student generation, which impresses me as one of its most characteristic and differentiating qualities. After continuous contact with ten student generations since my own, this one seems to me much the most serious-minded of them all. As I have watched them keep on discussing in little groups for hours after the meeting is over; forgetting even the meal hour sometimes in their absorption with some fundamental problem of which my contemporaries in college were hardly then aware: it has often struck me that our pre-war "age of confidence," and not least its student generations, were both complacent and superficial by comparison.

Related to this is another and very important change of mood among contemporary students, which the wife of a professor at Northwestern, in a well-remembered article in *Scribners* two or three years ago, called *"The Passing of Sophistication."* Those of us who well remember the period when the up-to-date and crushing student come-back to all the highest hopes and deepest faiths of humanity was either "Oh yeah!" or "So what?" are aware of a subtle but very significant change in the campus climate at this critical point. The brittle sophistication that was then so sure of the finality of its own cleverness or dogmatism has been lessened by the graduation of every senior class for several years past; and the incoming freshmen, not less intelligent or critical than their predecessors and sometimes more so, have at the same time not been ashamed to show considerably more of the native idealism of normal youth. They can still say "Oh yeah!" or "So what?" when either pretensions or traditionalism have to be debunked: but they do not echo it like parrots on all occasions. When religion is up for discussion, they are less disposed than their sophisticated predecessors to say with a shrug of the shoulders, "Nothing to it!" and much more ready to ask seriously, "What is there in it?"

This change of mood roots itself deeply of course in a new sense of the seriousness of our human situation, and of the precarious future of our boasted civilization. Here is "the great divide" between the mind of the present student generation and that of its pre-war predecessors. We had no question about the adequacy or the future of our democracy, our capitalistic social order, our civilization itself. When our faculty-student committee was considering together whom it should invite to our Chapel pulpit the following year, a senior remarked, "We want preachers who can tell us what is wrong with our civilization." Equally significant was the reply of an outstanding law student whom I had asked to explain the appeal of medieval philosophies to the modern student mind. "It grows out of our sense of insecurity as we look out and ahead. We listen gladly to anybody who tells us just what to think and do and believe, and offers to take the responsibility off our shoulders." This would explain the apparently increased influence and appeal of authoritarian types of both religion and theology to the modern mind—including even its students.

Deepest of all the factors in the quickened student interest in religion is the quest for primary values and ultimate faiths in a time when thoughtful youth, like its elders, feels its own inner inadequacy to the demands which such a time makes upon it. Dr. Stanley Jones reported after the first year of the University Missions that he was surprised to find, on returning from India, a spiritual sensitiveness and responsiveness among present-day students that was quite unlike the sophistication and superiority he remembered so well among their predecessors; but that he was struck by the fact that these same outreaching and often wistful students seemed to have no cause to which to give themselves, no ultimate faith commanding their supreme loyalty and devotion. His observation is related to that of Eduard C. Lindeman in his recent Jenkins Lecture in Chicago, that American youth today inclines to be sceptical—but not yet pessimistic. From the perspectives of "high religion" the attitudes of students tend to be those of questioning and questing —"What is there in it?"—but not so often those of all-out conviction, or what our fathers called "assurance."

The clearest exception to this rather risky generalization is probably to be found in certain areas of the widespread pacifism among American students. A recent *Fortune* poll indicated that whereas 34% of business men and 42% of all voters wanted to keep out of war no matter what happens abroad, 67% of college students were for keeping out at all costs. The point of view of these students has been stated by two of them with great clearness and restraint, and with candor and modesty, in the September *Atlantic*. There is no issue on which younger and older folk are more liable to fail to understand and so to misjudge each other as age groups, than on this one —as witness the recent cleavages between faculty and student opinion on many campuses. Among these 67%, the conviction of many springs from a sense of the futility of war as evidenced in history, and its social and spiritual waste and destructiveness as shown by the aftermath of the Great War: this attitude is sometimes disillusioned or even cynical, rather than positively religious in its motivation; a negative, or better a critical idealism, tending to inhibit action more than to inspire it. In many other students the pacifist attitude is positively and even sacrificially religious—a self-dedication at any personal cost to what is sincerely believed to be the will of God. Both the social idealism and the religion of students find some of their clearest and purest contemporary expressions in such pacifism. Much will depend for both the patriotism and the religion of the future, on whether those elders and contemporaries who cannot agree in the pacifist interpretation of contemporary issues recognize and seek to understand the genuine idealism that motivates it. Even more will depend upon the course of America's relation to the present war in the unpredictable months and years ahead: for those of us who remember the high hopes of spiritual revival that were so widely cherished when we entered the last war, and what actually happened afterward, especially to the younger generation that carried its chief burden, can cherish few illusions or even hopes on this point, if history should once more repeat itself.

III

In so far as these observations of current trends and these analyses of their causes are valid, they seem to point clearly toward certain conclusions as to the place of religion in higher education.

1. The need for adequate provision of competent instruction in the history and philosophy of religion in general, and of Christianity in particular, in the curricula of institutions both private and public, grows with the widening religious illiteracy in American life. This is due not simply to the fact that home and church no longer provide religious training for so large a proportion of American youth as in former years; but also to the deepening conviction among the younger as well as the older generation, that religious valuations and motivations are vital to the preservation and extension of both democracy and civilization. At a meeting of the Trustees of Princeton University on June 10, 1940, a report by the President on Princeton's religious program of public worship, practical service, and academic instruction, was accepted and approved. The following sentence is taken from the section on "the intellectual approach" through new courses and a new Professorship of Religious Thought, that are intended to develop into a Department of Religion:—

Princeton's historic position and present conviction and the acute needs of the time demand that we take vigorous steps to meet our responsibility of developing in our students a fuller understanding of religion and its significance.

Whether state institutions should meet this need by offering courses in religion themselves, as the University of Oregon now does, or by encouraging the development near the campus of independent religious foundations whose courses are recognized for credit, as at the University of Iowa and many others, may well depend upon public opinion in the particular state. But the responsibility for the provision of instruction in religion in some competent form rests upon all institutions of higher learning alike. The inevitable questionings, perplexities, and confusions of the growing mind of youth about its religious heritage and problems will most surely find their proper perspective and ultimate clarification when such untrammeled and scholarly instruction is not only officially provided, but widely elected by the students. For those who cannot take time for courses in religion, series of lectures by the faculty, like those which have had such surprising response at

Harvard in recent years, might well be offered. To make no provision or recognition for instruction in religion, as public education in America has usually done, will increasingly seem to thoughtful youth to imply that religion is unimportant in a democracy.

2. Since religious insights and convictions are more often caught from maturer personalities than they are deliberately taught in classrooms or elsewhere, it is important that college and university administrations give continuous attention to the maintenance on their faculties of a reasonable proportion of men and women who combine religious convictions and activity with professional competence in their own fields. The eager desire of present-day students for closer personal contacts with their faculties, so vigorously expressed of late on so many campuses, suggests the opportunity for informal discussion groups in faculty homes, as well as for personal conferences with interested professors, on religious questions. The outgrowing of immature religious conceptions, for the individual as for the race, is usually a slow and often a painful process; and for the wisest men, is shot through with perplexity and set within mystery. The best counsel can rarely solve such problems out of hand—for others as for one's self; but it can help immensely with maturer perspectives and the steadying encouragement of longer experience with religious perplexities.

At this point I record my own impression that the quickening of religious interest among students, of which this paper has made so much, is not in any comparable degree in evidence among our faculties, whose attitude in these matters by and large is what the familiar military phrase calls "as you were." I raise also the question whether a faculty generation that not only remembers as characteristic of students, but sometimes continues in itself, the attitudes of its own student days, is likely to be able to understand, much less to guide and help, the religious questing and wistfulness of this student generation, motivated as it is by a sense of social and personal urgency in these matters which we in our younger years rarely felt. Here, as so often, the gulf between the generations is deeper and wider than a friend of both could wish—even when the problems and difficulties of religious faith are equally felt on both sides of it.

3. The social nature of religion, and the motivations to

action which at its best it releases, make evident the central importance of religious group activities on and around a campus. Whether the direction of these is provided by the institution or by the neighboring churches, their vigorous and efficient functioning is indispensable for students, as for all other religious life; and the placing of a large measure of responsible leadership and self-determination of policy in the hands of students themselves, with competent counsel always available, is itself an important contribution both to the educational and to the democratic process.

The recognition that religion is at once a heritage from the past, a fellowship in the present, and a trust for the future, suggests the importance for higher education, as for all modern life, of a larger recognition of the religious community. For the Christian religion, with its emphasis on participation by the individual in a fellowship that is larger than that of race or class or country, or even of that of a single generation or of humanity by itself, the importance of the religious community is enhanced. Students of today may be more interested in religion than were their predecessors, but they are not less critical of the faults and failures of organized religion, especially of its provinciality and sectarianism; and they are very often in strong reaction against the church as they have seen it in their home town—especially when it is a small town. On the other hand, most church bodies are taking a far larger initiative in the maintaining of contacts with their own young people away at college; and the influence of the younger ministry on students seems to be increasing—in some student centers it is a powerful religious force. I have been impressed by the larger number of promising students who have sought me out for conference about the ministry within the last year or two. I like to believe that this may portend the further strengthening of the younger ministry, which many of us already account one of the hopeful signs in the contemporary church.

The note on which I close is that the place of religion in the higher education of youth must always have a forward-looking reference. My own observation has been that students do not fully appreciate either the values of religion or the functions of the church, until they get out of "preparation for life" into the "great essential experiences of human life," in business or profession, in marriage and parenthood, in all human relations. Graduates come back years afterward to say that they begin to see now, far better than in the undergraduate discussions of long ago, what religion is all about, and why the church is important both to them and to their children. So long as this longer time-span is of the essence of religious work with students, it will always be part of the function of religion in higher education to provide them with vital seeds, the blossom and full fruitage of which only the years and the generations afterward will reveal. With this longer perspective in view to explain and justify it, I reiterate my own conviction that with all its difficulties and some of its limitations what they unquestionably are, this present student generation "has the makings" of a more profound and vital religion than any previous student generation that I have personally known.

Religion and Action

By

REINHOLD NIEBUHR, D.D.*

MAN, as a living creature driven by the necessities of nature, is forced to act. Action is the essence of his existence. But man is no simple creature and is not simply contained within, and limited by, nature's impulses and necessities. He is a creature who transcends the natural process to which he is related. His rational freedom over natural process forces him to think as well as to act: to think in order to bring his action into conformity with some general scheme of purpose and some coherent system of ends.

But the freedom of man is not limited by the freedom of his reason over the processes of nature. It includes the spiritual freedom to transcend himself as well as to transcend nature. This higher freedom of self-transcendence may be included in what is usually designated as rational freedom. But if it is included, it must be clearly understood that the capacity of self-transcendence is a special dimension of freedom. Man as self-transcendent spirit stands outside of himself and his world, making both himself and the world the object of his contemplation. This higher dimension of freedom is the source of all religion. It forces human beings to relate their actions in the last resort to the totality of things conceived as a realm of meaning. Action which has become emancipated from nature's necessities remains incoherent until it has found a final anchor and source of coherence in a total realm of meaning. For this reason all action proceeds from and is oriented by a conscious or unconscious, an implicit or explicit religion, an overt or covert presupposition about the meaning of life.

The freedom of man and his capacity to make himself and the world the object of his thought not only constitutes his nature as "incurably religious" but it also forces him to seek

---

* William E. Dodge, Jr. Professor of Applied Christianity, Union Theological Seminary.

for a center and source of his system of meaning beyond himself and the world. Every system of meaning is rooted and grounded in a principle of meaning which is not the object but the presupposition of thought, which is not the consequence but the principle of rational analysis. This transcendent principle is the god of religion. To be sure it is possible for men to conclude that "nothing but" the causal sequences of nature give the world meaning. In that case we have a religion in which "nature" or "causality" is in effect God. It may be asserted that a rational analysis of the world has forced us to the conclusion that nature is God. But a careful scrutiny of the processes by which we arrive at this conclusion must lead to the conviction that the presupposition that nature is God was subtly involved in the reasoning by which we arrived at the conclusion. The system of nature is regarded as the ultimate principle of meaning. Such a conclusion is naturally subject to criticism. Is the system of natural causality really the ultimate principle of interpretation? Does it do justice to the element of novelty in the sequences of nature? Above all does it do justice to human freedom, to man's transcendence over nature? Does it not exclude what is most significant in human life from the system of meaning which has been established?

In the same manner it may be asserted that life and the world are meaningful only in terms of a rational coherence, in which case it is reason rather than nature which is regarded as God. Certainly there is no possibility of elaborating a realm of meaning without engaging the rational faculty. But if the rational faculty is itself made god, the question arises whether it is sufficiently ultimate to bear the burden of divinity. Can a man who transcends his own reason to such a degree as to be able to ask the question whether it is the ultimate and essential principle within himself and whether there is a significant coincidence between the processes of nature and the processes of mind, so that one may be sure that the mystery of mind unlocks the mystery of nature, can such a man really make reason into God? He may of course declare that it is not his reason but a more transcendent reason which is really God. But in that case he would have to be sure that what is connoted by "reason" was able to explain the world not only as a system of coherence but also as a realm of vitality. Premature identifications of rationality and meaningfulness always tend to depreciate action and vitality in favor of an imperturbable realm of forms.

However, we are not for the moment concerned with the task of measuring the adequacy of various types of religion and of various concepts of God. The immediate point is that men, who are driven by their nature as living creatures to act, are also compelled by their nature as free spirits to relate their actions to, and bring them into conformity with, some total scheme of meaning, and are furthermore prompted by the dimension of their freedom to seek for an ultimate source of meaning. There is no action without religious orientation and no religion without God. There are, of course, many actions in terms of immediate necessities which are not consciously related to a total scheme of meaning. But every man, in so far as he lives in some degree of freedom over nature, is bound to construct some kind of universe of meaning and to relate his actions into a scheme of coherence with this universe.

II

Ideally, religion is the force which brings all individual actions and vitalities into a total scheme of harmony by subjecting them all to the realm of meaning. Ideally, religion is the principle of harmony which must be substituted for the harmony of nature, once man's freedom has broken the latter and made the equanimity and order of nature unavailable for him. Yet religion is frequently (and some believe always) the force of disharmony in life. It accentuates conflict, generates fanaticism, and aggravates the pride and arrogance of individuals and groups. How is it that a principle of harmony should become a force of disharmony and conflict in actual history? Why is it that man has such great difficulty in bringing his actions into conformity with a total scheme of values? The simplest answer to these questions is that while religion is on the one hand the force which subjects all actions and vitalities to a total scheme of meaning, it is on the other hand the force which gives and creates false ultimates and false schemes of meaning. It relates the immediate to the ultimate; but when it centers life around a false ultimate, when it seeks to organize life around an inadequate center of meaning, a false god, it brings chaos into the world. The basic and perennial problem of religion is, in other words, the problem of idolatry. Men are not persuaded by any particular religion or by religion in general to worship false gods. But they are tempted by the situation in which they stand to use religion for the worship of false gods. The situation in which they stand is the situation of finiteness and freedom. They are on the one hand involved in the flux of nature and bound by its limits. On the other hand they transcend the flux of time and the limits of nature. They transcend their immediate situation to such a degree that they cannot act in it without bringing their actions into relation with some total structure of meaning. But they do not transcend their immediate situation sufficiently to be able to envisage the ultimate center and principle of meaning without filling it with content and connotations drawn from their immediate situation. In short, they conceive of God in their own image.

The anatomy of idolatry can be analyzed most clearly in the study of primitive religion. All primitive religion, whether animistic or totemistic, centers life prematurely around some vitality of nature or history, which is incapable of serving as a final center of meaning. Indeed primitive polytheism in its earlier forms has only an inchoate sense of a comprehensive system of meaning. It has many gods, which is an absurdity, since the very character of a god, even in polytheism, implies an unconditioned claim upon life. In the religious systems of the earlier empires of Egypt and Babylon we descern a certain order and comprehensiveness emerging out of the primitive chaos. In the pantheon of the gods, one god assumes a chief place. This chief god reveals both animistic and totemistic characteristics. Ra, the god of Egypt, is the god of the sun but he is also the god of Egypt. But before he was the god of Egypt he was the god of the city-state Heliopolis; and he achieved his superior position partly through the hegemony of this city-state in the unification of Egypt. If we disregard the animistic distractions or complications in the mosaic of imperial polytheism we note that what gradually emerges is a form of idolatry in which the god of Egypt is assumed to be something more than the god of Egypt. It is assumed that in some sense he is the transcendent source and end of all existence. This god is indeed more universal than the totemistic divinity of the primitive tribe; but on the other hand he also makes more pretentious universal claims than the tribal god. The gods of the early empires clearly reveal the ambiguous compound of universalism and imperialism, which is the perennial problem of man's spiritual life. The God of Egypt is something more than the god of Egypt. This is the symbol of finite man's recognition of a center and mystery of existence beyond the confines of his collective existence. Yet he is the God of Egypt, and what lies beyond Egypt in terms of life and value must be subordinated to Egypt by means of his universal claims. This is the symbol of finite man's effort to comprehend the ultimate in terms of the immediate.

This ambiguous character of religion is involved in all primitive brutalities and in the fanaticisms of imperial conflicts. These brutalities and conflicts are never merely expressions of natural vitality. Primitive man is brutal toward his foe, just as a modern self-righteous Pharisee is cruel toward his adversary not simply because "animal" passion has not been sufficiently disciplined by reason. This brutality in human history is spiritual and not natural. It results not from the chaos of natural impulses which have not yet been brought under the discipline of mind. It results from a spiritual chaos in which various vitalities and forces of nature and history are brought in conflict with each other because each seeks to usurp a position of superiority and centrality which is incompatible with its conditioned and finite character.

Religion is so deeply involved in the brutalities and conflicts of society that one can quite understand the viewpoint of rationalistic anthropologists, or for that matter rationalistic social scientists of any kind who, since the eighteenth century, have asserted that religion is a force of chaos and social disorder which must be eliminated from human history. But while one may understand such a viewpoint it is nevertheless a very superficial one. Religion is not some artifact of priests; and idolatry, the worship of contingent elements in history as the ultimate centers of meaning, is not some aberration of religion which could be eliminated if religion were destroyed. What is known as religion is simply man's effort to come to terms with his situation of finiteness and freedom. Since man transcends both nature and himself he is bound to seek for a principle of meaning which will give coherence to his world beyond nature and himself. Since man is finite and involved in nature he is bound to express his sense of the ultimate in less than ultimate terms. That is, he makes God in his own image and his god therefore comes in conflict with other gods made in the image of other men and other civilizations and cultures; and the conflict is brutal beyond the brutality of animal life because unconditioned claims are made for these conditioned values. This is a permanent and perennial problem of human history, and it reveals itself with equal clarity whether the religious element is explicit or only implicit, and whether men are consciously religious or have consciously disavowed traditional religion.

III

All high religions represent varying strategies for solving this problem of overcoming the chaos of human history and of bringing human actions into conformity with a general realm of order and coherent meaning. High religions may be divided into three types with reference to their solution of this problem. The first two of these three types are two versions of what may be generally designated as "culture religions" in distinction to the third type of religion, which is religion of revelation or prophetic religion. Culture religions seek by some discipline of heart or mind to extricate the soul and the mind from the welter of passion and the conflicts of nature and history in which it is involved. Both types of culture religion are united in their belief that the conflict of interest and the chaos of human action is due to the self's involvement in the passions and the necessities of nature. Both derive the evil in human history not from the freedom of the human spirit but from the inertia of man's physical nature. Both define the religious task as the extrication of the self from its involvement in nature by some internal discipline, whether rational or mystical, so that it will achieve perfect harmony or even identity with the eternal and transcendent realm of source of meaning, with God. The more rational versions of culture religion regard human reason as the agent of universality and order. The more mystical versions believe reason itself to be involved in finiteness, and seek to cultivate a discipline above the level of reason which will emancipate the soul from its involvement in nature, from its dependence upon the necessities and contingencies of the natural order. Despite the wide variety of mystical religions, the mystical technique may without unfairness be defined in comprehensive terms. It is the technique of introversion by which the self cuts its contacts with the outside world and centers consciousness upon the unity of consciousness in the belief that this inner unity of consciousness represents the divine principle within the self. The self achieves divinity, and finally even absorption into the divine, by destroying or obscuring the multiplicity, variety, and particularity of the finite world.

While a distinction must be made between the mystical and the rational versions of this ascent from particularity to universality, from finiteness to eternity, from confusion and conflict to order and peace, this distinction is neither absolute nor of primary importance. The more important distinction is between the pessimistic and optimistic, between acosmic and the cosmic versions of this strategy. There are pessimistic and world-denying forms of rationalism and mysticism which rest upon the basic assumption that the finite world is, as such, evil, and that the evil of human life is the inevitable consequence of the contingent, dependent, and insufficient character of human existence. What is born and derived is evil, according to Buddha. The finite world is neither evil or illusory. Salvation is defined as emancipation from this finite world. The Orient has developed this type of acosmism most consistently. Hinduism with its doctrine that Brahman and Atman are one reveals the technique of introversion most clearly. The soul in the deepest unity of its self-consciousness is one with God; and salvation is achieved by the introvert effort to reach this subliminal unity of the soul. Buddhism, with its doctrine of Nirvana as the final goal and end of life, reveals the logic of acosmic mysticism most clearly. Nirvana is significantly a state which can be defined neither in terms of existence or nonexistence. It hovers between them. It is a state in which all desire has been stilled and in which selfhood has been destroyed and all particularity has been transcended.

In all acosmic mysticism the soul uses the technique of introversion to project a ladder into the eternal, into the realm of undifferentiated unity of existence; and then it seeks to draw the ladder up after it. The finite world is regarded as evil by reason of the particularity and individuality of its discrete forms of life so that extinction is the only possible salvation.

In the western world, culture religions have never been able to reach a stable equilibrium between the pessimistic and the more optimistic versions of the belief that man's involvement in the necessities and contingencies of nature is the cause of evil and pain in human life. The more optimistic version does not seek flight into an undifferentiated eternity. It seeks rather to establish the eternal and the universal in history. It believes that human reason, or some mystic capacity above the level of reason, is capable of freeing the self from the bondage of nature. It does not regard contemplation and passivity as an end in itself. It believes that thought and contemplation may lift the self above the welter of passion and conflict of interest. It believes in the self-emancipation of man by the power of his rational faculties.

The classical culture of Greece betrays a significant ambiguity in its analysis of this problem. It is both pessimistic and optimistic, both world-affirming and world-denying in alternate moods. Plato wants reason to govern the world and the philosopher-king to bring order out of chaos in the city-state. But he has moments of pessimism in which he confesses that whether such a city as he envisages exists on earth or not does not matter. The roots of neo-Platonic world-denial are in Plato himself. The sober and naturalistic Aristotle, for whom nature is the footstool of the ultimate perfection, nevertheless defines the final blessedness as the contemplation of perfection. Here contemplation ceases to be preparation for harmonious action and becomes an end in itself. In the same way there is an equivocal note in Stoicism. It is on the one hand a rationalistic pantheism which seeks by the discipline of reason to bring all actions and passions into a system of harmony; but on the other hand stoic mysticism despairs of the world and prompts the self to withdraw into itself to secure that perfect imperturbability, that *ataraxia* and *apatheia* which is the consummation of stoic spirituality.

The note of ambiguity and equivocation between life-denial and life-affirmation, between contemplation as a method of extricating the self from the world and as a method of conquering the passions and the chaos of the world is thus a basic aspect of classical culture. To a certain degree it has been transmitted to our western culture. Yet on the whole the western world, partly under the influence of Hebraic and Christian forms of life-affirmation, has chosen the optimistic as against the pessi-

mistic form of culture religion. But the basis of its affirmative
attitude toward life is not, or has not always been, primarily
Hebraic or Christian. The basis is confidence in reason as a
force which will bring all the activities and vitalities of life
progressively under the dominion of a universal harmony. The
rational optimists agree with the pessimists in regarding man's
involvement in nature as the cause of his ills. But they disagree
with the pessimists in their estimate of reason, which is for
them not involved in finiteness and nature but the force of
universality by which man in history is extricated from the
partial and the particular.

We do not understand the history of our culture, particularly
since the Renaissance, if we do not recognize to what degree
ratio is really the god of modern western man. Reason is the
principle of meaning. It is also the force which subordinates all
vitalities to this principle. In the impressive system of Hegelian
idealism the whole of human history is conceived as a process
of man's gradual spiritualization. The essential conflict in
human nature is defined as the conflict between the self as
imbedded in "nature-necessity" and the rational and universal
self which must and can extricate itself from the too narrow
and limited objectives of nature. Hegel does not shrink from
identifying the element of universality in human reason with
the Absolute itself. In his thought the logic of rationalism
becomes crystal clear. Reason is not only God but the effective
agent of subduing all recalcitrant vitalities of history and nature
to its order and harmony. The tragic inadequacy of this solution of man's spiritual problem can be measured by analyzing
the social theories which flow from Hegel's thought. He finds
the state to be the real instrument of human salvation because
he regards its collective and comparatively universal character
as the historical expression of the universal principle in conflict
with particularity and individuality. Yet it is precisely in man's
collectve life that human conflict and fanaticism become most
destructive. Collective man engages in idolatrous self-worship
and makes pretentious denials of the contingent and partial
character of his existence which individual man cannot allow
himself because it would be impossible to make such idolatry
plausible. The realm of collective behavior is the very point at
which the spiritual pride of man makes its final most desperate

and most pathetic effort to obscure the weakness, dependence, and finiteness of human existence.

The worship of reason as God is not confined to idealistic rationalists. The most significant characteristic of modern culture is its tendency to press even naturalistic philosophies into the service of this religion. The naturalist may seek to interpret man primarily in terms of his relation to nature, and may minimize his rational transcendence over natural process. Yet he curiously places his faith in reason as the seat of virtue. Thus in the philosophy of Professor Dewey reason has only a limited freedom over the impulses of nature, but that does not prevent him from manifesting the most touching faith in the ability of "free coöperative inquiry" to achieve a vantage point of disinterested intelligence from which it can arbitrate and harmonize the conflicting interests of men. In effect, even the naturalist regards the limited ends of natural impulse as the cause of confusion in human life and hopes that the more universal objectives of reason will bring harmony and coherence into all human activity.

It must be observed that there has always been a note of scepticism in modern culture about this worship of reason. The romantic movement has been the bearer of this scepticism. In some of its forms (as for instance in the philosophy of Bergson) it calls attention to the fact that nature has its own system of harmony which the "divisiveness" of reason destroys. It discovers, in other words, that human freedom breaks the harmony of nature and does not find it easy to achieve a higher and better harmony. In some of its forms romanticism expresses the fear that a rational harmonization of impulse will destroy and enervate the vitality of natural impulse. This is the burden of Nietzsche's protest against rationalism. This form of romanticism is afraid that the "harmony of the whole will destroy the vitality of the parts" (Santayana), that *Fleiss in den Formen kann zuweilen die massive Wahrheit des Stoffes vergeszen lassen* (Schiller). A third form of romantic protest, as it is developed by Marxist materialism and by psychoanalytic psychology particularly, expresses no fears that reason may enervate impulse; it has the contrary conviction that reason is really the servant of impulse and that its pretensions of mastery are bogus. The Marxist calls attention to the ideological character of all human culture and to the intimate relation between interest and the supposedly transcendent and disinterested conclusions of philosophy, religion, and law. The psychologist reveals this same tendency toward rationalization in more intimate and individual terms.

There is a negative validity in all these romantic criticisms of rationalism. It is not as easy to lift human action into a realm of complete harmony with all conflicting vitalities as rationalism assumes. The bigotry of cultures is not due merely to the limited vision of ignorance. Race prejudice is not simply dissolved by enlarging intelligence until it envisages the values and interests of other races. Injustice is not merely the consequence of the failure to include the interest of the other in the field of vision; or of a faulty logic which fails to concede a value to others which it claims for the self. The romantic protest (in which Marxism must be included, despite the fact that it is only provisionally romantic and ultimately develops a rationalism of its own) rightly calls attention to the fact that human reason is never the transcendent force of disinterestedness which it pretends to be. It is more intimately and organically related to human passions and interests than the rationalist realizes. Reason, like idolatrous religion, does not simply subordinate the immediate to the ultimate and the partial to the universal. Its effect is always partly to give the immediate the prestige of the absolute and to veil the partial behind the universal. The idolatrous tendency of man to make his own life, culture, civilization, race, nation, and interest the premature center of the whole world of meaning is not so simply overcome by rational contemplation and discipline as the optimistic version of rationalism assumes. This is why a rationalistic bourgeois civilization which began with such high hopes of achieving a universal culture and establishing universal peace is perishing today in a welter of bigotry and international anarchy.

Yet the romantic protest against rationalism does not solve the problem of human spirituality. If the vitality of nature is asserted against the enervation of reason we are left without a principle of harmony to discipline the supernatural vitalities of man. Some romanticism leads to nihilism. If the unity of nature is asserted against the divisiveness of mind we are left with no principle of harmony but the inadequate forces of cohesion in nature itself, the principle of consanguinity in politics, for instance. This form of romanticism leads to primitivism. If romanticism merely challenges reason's pretensions of mastery over natural impulse, the question still remains unsolved how man is to achieve either internal or social harmony.

These weaknesses of romanticism prove that it is not possible to solve the human problem by emphasizing the sub-rational vitalities and unities in man, once we have discovered that we cannot explain human behavior merely by emphasizing his rational faculties. The fact is that the confusion in human life is not due to the limited objectives of natural impulse as rationalism assumes; but neither can it be cured by a simple disavowal of the freedom and capacity for the transcendence involved in man's rational faculties. The real situation is that man does transcend nature, but he also transcends himself. He is therefore capable of using and debasing the universal aspects of reason to make them tools of his own interest. The sense of coherence and consistency in reason is, in short, no adequate guarantee of a disciplined human freedom. The man who transcends nature is not so simply the servant of reason as rationalism assumes. Reason is on the one hand a force of transcendence which brings the interests of the self into a field of coherence with the interests of others. It is on the other hand an instrument by which the self makes itself the center of such a system of coherence. Immanuel Kant recognized this in his theory of "radical evil," though this recognition stood in contradiction to his total system of thought and would have annihilated his whole philosophy of morals, had he elaborated it.

There is in short no solution for the human problem in terms of so-called "culture religion." Pessimistic culture religions are really closer to the truth than the optimistic versions because they recognize that the same *ratio*, the same principle of *logos* in man which presumes to achieve universality and transcendence is itself involved in finiteness and actually aggravates the human problem by pretending a degree of transcendence which is beyond the capacities of finite man. But pessimistic culture religions have no solution for the historical problem of man. They merely negate history. The optimistic versions of culture religion betray us into utopian illusions, which historical reality consistently disappoints. We are now living in a period of history in which we are subjected to the most tragic disillusionment of these utopian hopes.

IV

Is there any escape from the dilemma of either disavowing the world of historical reality because it is involved in contingency and finiteness or of establishing false and premature absolutes in it, thereby aggravating its chaos and confusion? In answering that question we must look finally at biblical religion which belongs in a separate category of religion. It not only offers a different solution for the problem of human spirituality but it defines the problem in very distinctive terms. For biblical religion, God, who is the source and end of all existence, is more completely transcendent than the God of culture religion. He is not merely the *logos*, the principle of form which brings the formless stuff into order. He is the Creator who is the source of both form and vitality. His *word* is not an impersonal form and principle of order. It is a creative act. "God spake and it was done." "God said, let there be light, and there was light." These assertions reveal the typical biblical conception of divine transcendence in which the creative *act* is definitive for the divine nature. God created the world. The world is not, as in neo-Platonic mysticism, an emanation from the divine and transcendent unity of life. The world is therefore not evil by reason of its involvement in contingency and finiteness. Man is not evil by reason of his physical existence. Sin does not spring from nature. Human acts are not involved in evil because they are bound by the limits of nature.

The biblical conception of God as Creator and the doctrine of the goodness of creation lead to a very significant consequence in the definition of the human situation. Man is a creature but he is not evil by reason of the finiteness of his existence. He is a creature in every sense, which is to say that he is not divine in his rational life and a creature only in his physical life. His rational capacities are not an eternal element which must be extricated from the finite and the natural element.

Yet biblical religion does not conceive the human situation as modern naturalism does. It does not define man primarily in terms of his relation to nature. It declares that man is made in the image of God. While the term *imago Dei* is variously defined, sometimes in terms which equate it with the mere idea of "reason," the general tendency of Christian thought is to emphasize that the image of God in man is a capacity for transcendence. Man is, in other words, a creature who cannot understand himself either in terms of his relation to nature or yet in terms of his rational transcendence over nature. He can understand himself only as he is understood from beyond himself, from the standpoint of God. His capacity for self-transcendence in infinite regression means that he cannot comprehend himself without a principle of comprehension which is beyond his comprehension. Yet it is believed that the God who is this principle of comprehension makes himself known to man. That is why biblical religion is a religion of revelation. It does not believe that it is possible for finite man to comprehend the transcendent and eternal. But it does believe that finite man is able to accept by faith the significant revelations in time and history of what lies beyond time and history and gives history meaning.

Ideally this would mean that men are able by faith to bring all their impulses into conformity with one another and to relate their interests and actions harmoniously to the interests and actions of others when they had found the transcendent source and center of life's meaning which can alone dictate this harmony. All lesser centers of meaning create confusion in human life and action because they lift a finite and contingent factor or force into the false eminence of life's center. There are forms of Christian gnosticism which regard this ideal possibility as a simple possibility. To them Christ has revealed God to man; and man once in the possession of the knowledge of the true God henceforth lives in obedience to His will. Most forms of modern liberal Christianity are touched with this gnostic heresy.

Christianity in its profounder forms does not regard this ideal possibility as a simple possibility at all. For it historical reality must be defined not only in terms of the two categories of man's creatureliness and his freedom (*imago Dei*) but also in terms of a third category, that of original sin. Man is child of God, creature and sinner. His sin is not the inertia of his physical nature upon the universal and inclusive ends which his reason projects. His sin springs from his spiritual capacities and is defined as pride and self-glorification. "He changes the glory of the incorruptible God into the image of corruptible man." (Romans I.) Unfortunately the concept of original sin has been confused in all Christian orthodoxy by the literal interpretation of the Fall as an historical event. But this literalism cannot entirely obscure the profound truth which underlies the biblical conception of sin. Sin is not the inertia of the partial against the claims of the universal. Sin is not the limited objective of nature against the inclusive end of spirit. Sin is the pride of finite man, who is not altogether finite but forgets how finite he is. Sin is not man's ignorance, but his refusal to admit his ignorance. Sin is not man's dependence upon natural necessity, but his refusal to admit his insecurity in nature and his consequent effort to establish complete security, that is, his lust for power. Sin is occasioned by the paradoxical human situation of finiteness and freedom, of involvement in nature and transcendence over nature. Sin is not expressed in the fact that no man is universal man, but American man or bourgeois man or western man. Sin is revealed in the fact that western man, or bourgeois man, or American man refuses to admit the partiality of his viewpoints and the contingent character of his existence. The human act is brutal not with the brutality of nature. Its brutality has a spiritual source. Man is ruthless with his foe because he regards his relative standards as absolute and must therefore regard the standards which do not conform to his own as evil.

It may be possible for man to be conscious of this dilemma in moments of transcendent contemplation. He may have an uneasy conscience when he contemplates the implicit pride and arrogance of his life. But this does not prevent him from continuing to sin in his actions. No rational universalism can save man from the sin of imperialism in action. The fact is that all actions are curiously compounded of universalism and imperialism. Man actually uses the universal perspective of his freedom partly as a false front and rationalization of his partial interest in action. This is the element of original sin in all historic activity. It is easy to see that biblical religion defines problems of historical action in more tragic terms than in any culture religion. It declares in effect that man is involved in a situation from which he cannot extricate himself by his own power. Every effort on his part to do so actually involves him more deeply in sin, since every such effort will merely insinuate the partial and particular perspective of finite man into the concept of the universal or the eternal which he projects. This process may be pitched upon higher and higher levels of culture. A genuine difference between primitive bigotry and civilized tolerance cannot be denied. But there is no level upon which man escapes the vicious circle. At the precise moment when he claims to have escaped the vicious circle he is most deeply involved in it. This is the tragedy of self-righteousness to which Jesus calls attention in the parable of the Pharisee and the Publican. It is the tragedy revealed in modern communist spirituality in which the communist begins by calling attention to the element of pretension in bourgeois culture and ends by claiming to have achieved a transcendent and absolute form of social justice.

What is the solution which biblical faith offers for this problem? What possible solution is adequate for a problem so grave? The solution for biblical religion is to be found in its doctrine of "grace." "With man this is impossible, with God all things are possible," said Jesus when his analysis of the situation of the rich young ruler had prompted his disciples to the despairing exclamation: "Lord who then can be saved!"

The biblical doctrine of grace is corollary to the doctrine of original sin and has meaning only in relation to it, which is why it has no meaning for modern Christians of the liberal tradition, who do not take the doctrine of original sin seriously. According to the Bible, history and revelation reach their climax in Christ, in whom the mercy of God is revealed. Christ is the final revelation of God because his suffering is a revelation of a redemptive resource in the heart of the divine which transcends punishment. All human history is involved in the tragedy of punishment because every culture and civilization, every individual and collective human enterprise "exalts itself above measure" and is destroyed. This tragedy of human history can be resolved only if the Eternal takes the contradictions of history into Himself. God suffers with and for man. Christ is thus the act of self-disclosure of God in history. He is the divine *logos*. At the Cross human history comes to a full realization of the perennial contradiction in which it stands. Man recognizes not only that he cannot be his own end, but that he cannot be saved from the abortive effort of making himself his own end without a divine initiative which overcomes this rebellion in his heart.

According to biblical doctrine Christ becomes not only the
"wisdom of God" which fully reveals the meaning of life. He
also becomes the "power of God," who fulfills life's meaning.
It is possible, if man is able to comprehend his situation in faith
and repentance, to appropriate resources beyond himself, by
which the sinful contradiction of his life is overcome. The
emphasis upon "grace" in Christian thought is always an antidote to the emphasis upon *gnosis* in classical and mystical
thought. The difference between the two is twofold. On the
one hand, the power of redemption is believed to come from
God and not man in the doctrine of grace. On the other hand,
it is power and not knowledge which is desired and obtained.
The prayer of the modern poet:

> Knowledge I ask not, knowledge thou hast sent
> But Lord the will, there lies my bitter need,

is completely orthodox. It analyzes the human situation exactly
as St. Paul does: "The will indeed is present with me, but how
to perform that which is good I know not." The claim of the
Christian doctrine of grace is that the soul which has become
contritely conscious of the fact that the deed always falls short
of the intent, that the justice which we achieve in action always
corrupts the scheme of justice which we conceive in contemplation, that the soul which knows itself incapable of transcending
the contradiction within itself between the divine will and self-
will, is given a measure of power not its own. The self as centered in itself is destroyed so that the self which is centered in
God may arise. St. Paul explains the process of regeneration in
the words: "I am crucified with Christ, nevertheless I live."
This is to say that redemption consists not in the destruction of
the self and its absorption into divinity or transcendent unity.
The particular and individual self is not destroyed. The self, on
the contrary, is more fully realized as it ceases to realize itself
too narrowly with itself as the center. The self as infinitely self-
transcendent can realize itself fully only as God becomes the
center of its life.

All Christian doctrines of sanctification rest upon this scriptural, more particularly Pauline, doctrine of grace as power,
of the divine fulfillment of life. Yet it must be noted immediately that there is another emphasis in Pauline thought from
which the Christian doctrine of justification, in distinction to

the doctrine of sanctification, is derived. According to this doctrine, Christ is not so much the power in us as the revelation of the divine mercy toward us. The symbol of salvation is not *Christus in nobis* but *Chirstus pro nobis*. The relation between a divine power which overcomes sin in actual history and of a divine power which overcomes sin by taking it into itself is not completely clear in Pauline thought. The proof that this is so is that St. Paul is the fountain and source of sanctificationist and perfectionist interpretations of history just as much as he is the source of the Reformation's emphasis upon justification.

The conflict between these two interpretations of sin and grace, which came to a head in the Reformation, is of tremendous importance for an understanding of the human situation. It has not been understood or considered important for the reason that modern forms of Christianity, following the general utopianism of modern culture, are so simply sanctificationist and perfectionist that the problem which the Reformation raised is completely irrelevant to them. The Reformation was a protest against the Catholic doctrine which subordinated justification to sanctification and claimed that whatever the sin of natural man might be, the redeemed man who had benefited from the infusion of sacramental grace was essentially perfect. It was not claimed that he achieved completion but that he "walked perfectly toward perfection" (St. Augustine). Catholic conceptions of redemption and sanctification establish a place in history, namely the church, in which sin is actually overcome. It is the contention of the Reformation that whenever such a claim is made the sin which is ostensibly overcome is actually expressed upon a new and more subtle basis. An historical institution, involved in the relativities and contingencies of nature and history, claims to have achieved a position of complete transcendence in history and by that very claim reveals the character of original sin in its most essential form; for it obscures partial and relative interests behind the aura of ultimate sanctity. Both Protestants and secularists, when observing the Papacy operating in the relativities of current European politics, and being tempted to come to terms with Fascist tyranny if only this tyranny does not try to destroy the church, think they can detect a striking verification of the Reformation criticism in current history. No religion lends itself so completely as an instrument of human pride as a religion in which this pride is broken in principle but in which the principle is used by finite man to make claims which transcend finiteness.

It is the affirmation of the Reformation, on the other hand, that the church, that the center of Christian faith, is the locus in history where the sin and pride of man is broken in principle but not in fact. This affirmation rests squarely upon those elements in Pauline thought in which grace is interpreted not as a power which overcomes the contradiction of sin in man but as the divine mercy which accepts man despite his sin. "The just shall live by faith." There is no locus in history where sin is overcome except in principle and in intention. There is no possible goodness in man which can give man an easy conscience. An easy conscience which rests upon moral achievement leads to moral pride on a higher and more terrible level.

This Protestant doctrine is the stone which the builders have rejected and which must become again the head of the corner. Modern liberal Protestantism has rejected the doctrine much more completely than medieval Christianity ever did. As a consequence it is involved in all the utopian illusions of modern culture. It regards perfect love as a simple possibility of history. In consequence it is always tempted to either Pharisaism or futility. Either it must say, as liberal Christianity said in the World War, that democracy is identical with the Kingdom of God, or it must say, as it is inclined to say now, that we cannot defend democracy because it is not just enough to deserve defense. Utopianism must either persuade itself that it has achieved a vantage point of perfection from which it can act, or it cannot act at all. This is to say that it is a source of either fanaticism or futility in the relativities and contingencies of history. Modern Christianity thinks it makes a tremendous contribution to politics when it insists that no one comes to the struggle against modern tyranny "with clean hands." Such an assertion can only imply that it would be possible for some individual or nation to achieve guiltlessness. This is exactly what is not possible.

All human actions remain within the limits of sin. "Every deed," says Nietzsche, "must be loved more than it deserves to be loved in order to be born." Nietzsche of course glorifies the sinful element in the deed because he is afraid of the enervation of moral scruples. In this he is wrong, but no more in error than those who think they can achieve guiltlessness by just a little more contemplation.

Whatever decency we establish in history, and whatever justice we are able to maintain against the threat of tyranny on the one hand and anarchy on the other, must rest upon a religious interpretation which refuses to make sin normative but which also refuses to withdraw from history because all history is sinful. "Sin bravely," said Luther. While it must be admitted that the evils of antinomianism lurk in this advice of Luther, it must be recognized that the evils of utopian Pharisaism and futility are implicit in perfectionist doctrines which do not understand the truth in this advice.

The Church as an Organ of Social Ideals

By

RUFUS M. JONES, Litt.D., D.D., Th.D., LL.D.[*]

WILLIAM JAMES in *Varieties of Religious Experience,* defined religion as "the feelings, acts and experiences of individual men *in their solitude,* so far as they apprehend themselves to stand in relation to whatever they may consider the Divine."[1] Speaking a little earlier in the same book of the contribution which the Quaker, George Fox, made to modern religious life, James speaks of it as "a religion of veracity *rooted in spiritual inwardness.*"[2] He apparently finds it to be "a religion of veracity" because it is "rooted in spiritual inwardness." He makes no account of the Quaker contribution to social transformations. Religion is "inwardness," not efforts to make a better "outwardness."

In a similar strain, Professor Whitehead has in quite recent times boldly defined religion "as what the individual does with his own solitude." In an earlier sentence Whitehead says with equally emphatic stress: "Religion is the art and the theory of the internal life of man, so far as it depends on the man himself, and on what is permanent in the nature of things," which last phrase we may assume means God. "This Doctrine," Whitehead comments, "is the direct negation of the theory that religion is primarily a social fact."[3]

There is, of course, a certain element of truth in this extreme position of Whitehead and James. Rudolf Otto with his theory of religion as the unique numinous feeling aroused in the soul, and Karl Barth with his conception of man's soul miraculously confronted in an utterly perpendicular way by the recreative act of a Divine Other, would both of them, I think, give back-

---

[*] Professor Emeritus of Philosophy, Haverford College; Chairman of American Friends Service Committee.

[1] *Varieties of Religious Experience,* p. 31.

[2] *Ibid.,* p. 7.

[3] All these quotations are from A. N. Whitehead, *Religion in the Making* (New York, 1926), p. 16.

ing to this view that religion, in its *essentia*, is what man does, or what is done to him, as "a solitary being," alone with God.

It is, of course, true in the last resort that whatever is perceived in this world, or felt, or thought, or apprehended, or appreciated, is perceived, or felt, or thought, or apprehended, or appreciated by *somebody in particular*, and not by some mysterious synthetic fusion of minds above or beyond the mind of the individual person who is the agent. We have schools of thought and movements in art and sects in religion, but in the final analysis we must go to the individual mind to explore the conscious experiences in each one of these fields.

But, nevertheless, there is only a tiny fraction of truth in this attempt to reduce religion to what one does alone with God in one's solitariness. The primary fact of human life is not the lonely individual, but the group that makes the individual possible. There can no self emerge in this world without a mother, without a purveyor of food; there can be no acquisition of language, no nurture of mind or spirit, no formation of ideals, no basis of reality without some kind of background society. Society of some sort is the primitive fact. One person alone is simply nobody at all. An isolated being with no relationships would be more difficult to find than the "missing link," and when found would contribute nothing to the meaning of life. Only in a madhouse can one find a completely isolated self. It is no more insane to conceive oneself composed of glass, or to be Ursa Major, than it is to expect to arrive at any goals of life apart from others. The unit-member is dependent at almost every point upon the community, upon the social group, that is, upon the life of the whole.

Religion, which is as immemorial as smiling and weeping, does not begin with a St. Stylites alone on the top of a pillar. If it had so begun the saint would soon have perished without a sympathetic community to feed him—or what is more important, to admire him. It is foolish for us to waste any precious time trying to settle the issue whether religion originates with the individual or with the group. It is as absurd as trying to find a stick which has only one end, or a board so thin that it has only one side. Individual and group cannot be cut apart and be treated as though either were real as a sundered existent.

The moment an individual has arrived on the scene with a capacity for the mystical, that is, the direct personal, apprehension of God and capacity to interpret his experience, there is bound to be behind this individual the long molding processes of history, the accumulations of the experiences and transmissions of many generations. If the given individual runs on ahead of the group, as a prophet-genius does do, it will be along the lines and in the direction for which the group has long been preparing the line of march. And the individual does not possess his insight with a permanent assurance until he has interpreted it and carried others along with his conviction. In short, however important the creative insight of the rare soul may be, religion does not count as a contribution to the race until a beloved community is formed and the discovery is interpreted and transmuted into a social movement. As far as its *significance* is concerned, religion is essentially *social*. It is an affair of a beloved community. Here I align myself with Josiah Royce rather than with William James, both of whom gave me their guidance and friendship.

St. Paul was not exaggerating when he declared that the church-group is Christ's body—the new body which is to be the living expression and growing interpretation in the world of the mind and spirit of Christ through the ages. And St. John is only stating what was literally the truth when he has Christ say of the new fellowship, "I am the vine-stock and you are the vine-branches of one living organism." There never was a time when Christianity was a disembodied idea, or ideal, or spirit. The Gospel itself was formulated and came to the world through the beloved community, and Christianity has always lived on and has always been transmitted through the Body of believers we call the Church.

I shall mean then, by *the Church* in this essay the Body of Christian believers and transmitters of Christ's mind and spirit through the centuries, rather than a specific organization, or institution, or a single concrete communion; however extensive or historically important. This larger, all-inclusive body of believers has sometimes been called the Church Universal, or what the Spiritual Reformers in the sixteenth century called the "Invisible Church," or in St. Augustine's famous phrase the *Civitas dei qualis nunc in terra*—the City of God as it now is on earth.

This continuous unbroken invisible Church of the Ages as the total Body of Believers has always been a social and socializ-

ing force in the world. It has always expressed its truth, its
spiritual message, in terms of a society. Its saints have not usually
been "exhibits" on lonely pillars; they have been men and
women living in the world and expressing in life and action
the ideals of their faith as they held it at the time. The Church
has always been a society of people living in the midst of the
world, penetrated by certain convictions about life. Even in
periods when no one yet talked of a "social gospel" in the modern sense, Christianity was nevertheless an immense constructive and socializing force in the world. It is well-nigh impossible
to overrate the importance of this constructive and socializing
force in the reconstruction of the Western World after the
overthrow of the Roman Empire by the hordes of the barbarian
invaders. The *Civitas dei* went right on as an operative power
when the visible empire was submerged, and built the new
epoch.

The thirteenth century, again, was one of the great birth
periods in Christian history. The century opened with the
apparent supremacy of the historic Church all but universally
recognized. But very early in the century it became evident
that nothing which is established in this world of mutability is
permanently, finally, fixed and settled. Just when the great
institution seemed to be most secure, powerful new currents
began to circulate, and fresh movements of the human spirit
invaded the established order. Some of the movements came
from within the Church itself and some of them had an anti-
Church animus and were plainly heretical, though more or less
under the spell of the New Testament.

Almost every one of the new movements of that creative
century, whether loyal to the Church or heretical in color, was
a passionate effort to widen the scope of life and to produce a
social order more in conformity with the Spirit of Christ and
the ideals of the New Testament. The Waldenses were among
the earliest exponents of the aim at simplicity of life and complete conformity to the Sermon on the Mount. The Sisterhoods
of Beguines and Brotherhoods of Beghards rapidly spread over
most of the area of the Western Church. They were sometimes
approved by the Church and sometimes condemned, but whether
approved or condemned, they worked assiduously to relieve suffering and to spread a spirit of human love and service. There
were many other brotherhood groups which came to birth in

this fertile century, invariably exhibiting the social passion of the period.

But beyond question the Franciscan movement, with its three Orders, was by far the most important event of the century in its bearing upon new social ideals and methods. The outstanding feature was the birth of a new spirit of love, a new human passion, and a positive effort to bring the world back to the way of life of the great Galilean.

The Protestant Reformation in the sixteenth century, along the main line of its movement, was profoundly theological in its emphasis, but it came to birth in a period of the Renaissance when aspirations for the liberation and enlargement of human life were working in men's minds and when there were powerful yearnings for social and economic changes. This deeper strain of life found expression in the little groups of Spiritual Reformers of the sixteenth century and in the somewhat chaotic types of Anabaptists. These eager radical reformers were defeated in their aspirations at the moment, but their ideals, like the ideals of most so-called "lost causes," emerged into life again and have found expression in modern democracies, in the Declaration of Independence, in the Constitution of the United States, and in the social aspirations of most American Churches. In fact many of the present-day religious denominations, including the Baptists and the Quakers, emerged out of these movements.

In more modern times the evangelical movement, which began with the Wesleys and Whitefield in the eighteenth century, and which in the end profoundly affected the Anglican Church, and eventually penetrated with a new devotion almost all branches of Christianity, was throughout its period a powerful social agency. It produced the great wave of foreign missionary effort around the globe. It brought new hope into the prisons of Europe and America. It aroused a new interest in the welfare of children. It produced the impulse which ended the slave trade and freed the slaves in all the colonies of Great Britain. The ameliorating influence of the Evangelical Awakening continued throughout the nineteenth century, like a warm gulf stream, and new and powerful forces came into play in the Victorian Era which created fresh hopes and expectation for the human race. The primary emphasis was no doubt put

on the salvation of the individual soul, but the total effect was
the formation of new and nobler ideals for human society.

Kant's categorical imperative that persons are always to be
treated as ends and never to be used as means or tools or instruments was one factor in the formation of the new outlook.
Rousseau and the Romanticists gave widespread vogue to the
fundamental rights of man and to belief in an innate goodness
in human nature until it was spoiled by the corruptions of
society. Auguste Comte with his "religion of humanity" and
Fourier with his scheme of phalansteries helped to produce the
new social atmosphere. As evolutionary philosophy expanded,
especially under the guidance of Herbert Spencer, the ultimate
perfection of man seemed to be assured. The Victorian poets
took up the vision and gave wings to the growing hopes. Meantime, the fresh studies of history recovered the stages of development of the religion of the Old Testament and brought the
Gospels, the Apostolic Age and the birth and expansion of the
Church into a new perspective.

The first effect of the doctrine of evolution and of the higher
critical study of the Scriptures was to produce widespread fear
and confusion in Christian circles, and many foolish books of
defense were written. They are fortunately so dead now that
they concern only the laborious historian. But this era was in
the main a period of hope and adventure, and creative and
constructive forces soon came strongly into play. Books began
to appear interpreting the social ideals of the great Hebrew
prophets as a new order of statesmen, and then a group of
awakened scholars led the thought of the Church in a series of
books on the "Social Gospel." While one group of scholars was
reporting the Gospels to be charged with apocalyptic and escha-
tological meaning, intended to prepare minds for the crisis of
the shift from an old-world order to a wholly new and utterly
different age, these Social Gospel writers were finding in the
New Testament the Magna Charta and the basic principles of
a Christian Society to be progressively realized by the leaders
of the Church. Charles Kingsley, Theodore T. Munger, Wash-
ington Gladden, and many other liberal thinkers and writers
and preachers prepared the way for this new Social Gospel.

Shailer Mathews, who for almost half a century has been a
foremost interpreter of the Social Gospel, began his long line

of books in 1897 with *The Social Teaching of Jesus.* A more
important book, perhaps the most important in the list of books
on this subject, was Francis Greenwood Peabody's *Jesus Christ
and the Social Question,* which was published in 1900. Henry
Churchill King of Oberlin comes next in the order with his
extremely vital book, *Theology and the Social Consciousness.*
Walter Rauschenbusch of Rochester, New York, came a little
later into the field, but he was more nearly the flaming prophet
of the movement than any other person. His first book on the
Social Gospel was *Christianity and the Social Crisis* (1908),
followed by *Dare We Be Christians* in 1914; *Social Principles
of Jesus* in 1916; and *A Theology for the Social Gospel* in 1917.
During these years Shailer Mathews was producing in succession
a long list of books on the Social Gospel, while many writers
were interpreting the Kingdom of God as a new progressive
Social Order. Perhaps my *Social Law in the Spiritual World*
(1904) might be mentioned in this connection.

The literature on the Social Gospel has become during the
forty years of this century a vast output of Sibylline leaves.
Preachers all over the land have preached this Gospel, and the
religious press has given it a wide vogue. Many churches have
under the spell of it become centers of social activity. To the
future historian of this period the social emphasis will almost
certainly appear as the most striking characteristic of the Christianity of this time, as evangelism was the characteristic mark of
the last quarter of the preceding century.

Meantime the stricter, the more realistic and technical higher
critical scholars have not been slow in sounding a caveat to this
social gospel movement. They fail to find a social program in
the Gospels. They do not endorse the view that the Kingdom
of God as taught in the New Testament was thought of as something to be realized through the socializing processes of Church
activities. They see Christ mainly concerned to produce a new
type of person rather than a new social reorganization. It is not
difficult to show, as these scholars have been doing, that the
Gospels came out of a peculiar psychological climate of the first
century in a world of a rural type with no intimation, or fore-
cast, of the complicated industrial and capitalistic problems of
our time. These problems, they tell us, are not anticipated in
the Gospels, and there is no program proposed there for dealing

with such far-away problems. The so-called social gospel is consequently, they insist, read back into the documents rather than actually *found* there and divinely transmitted to us. They find, too, a profound apocalyptic element in the Gospels which makes it seem impossible to their minds to apply the so-called teachings of the Gospels to the situations of the twentieth century.

But the interesting fact is that these Gospels which we possess cannot be "fixed" and reduced to static documents to be read forever in the light of a far-away bygone age. They are vital and dynamic and have a growing life with the life of the race. In spite of the failure of apocalyptic hopes, in fact in a large degree *because* of the failure of apocalyptic hopes, the Church grew and spread and conquered the Empire. If, as the "form critics" claim, the Church produced the Gospels, it is at least equally true that the Gospels have produced the Church as we now know it, and its life is interfused and interpenetrated with the inspiration and power of these books; they have grown in significance with the growth of the ages.

We may ask, and we do ask historically, what the "fathers" meant in the various sections of our American Constitution, but the Supreme Court in its wisdom, when peradventure it is wise, interprets that Constitution to meet the growing needs and the new unforeseen situations which arise in the life of an ever moving civilization. The Gospels fortunately are not legal documents. They are marked by a high quality of inspiration. They have come out of very high levels of life and are extraordinarily adapted to meet the issues of life in worlds undreamed of when they were written and for situations remote from the first century.

The Church will not be too much bound, I hope, by proof texts in our Scriptures, or search too much for legal warrant, as it goes forward to meet its spiritual tasks in these new and complex epochs of the world. The Church of the ages is a stream which began in mighty Head-waters, and it has until today kept its onward flow more or less influenced on great occasions by fontal tides of the Spirit. It can continue its mission, its divine function in the world, only as it discovers how to minister in some adequate way both to the souls and the bodies of men. There can be no significant continuing Church,

which is concerned solely with what is to happen eschatolog-
ically in a post-mortem sphere beyond the glimpses of the moon.
The Church must face the real issues of life and make a practical difference in the lives of actual men and women and children, or it is doomed to become a disappearing affair. That
does not mean that it is to become secularized. A completely
secularized Church has already reached its terminus, and its
mission as a Church of Christ is over.

The primary function of a Church, if it is to be a continuing
Body of Christ in the world, is to raise human life out of its
secular drift and to give reality to the eternal here in the midst
of time. When it ceases to bear witness to the real presence of
an eternal reality operating in and upon the lives of men, its
race is run; it has missed its mission. But just as certainly the
Church is commissioned as the organ of the Spirit to bring
health and healing to the human lives of men and to the social
order in which these lives are formed and molded.

It may be true, as the realistic higher critics tell us, that the
Kingdom of God as presented in the Gospels is not a new social
order to be slowly, painfully, and creatively realized here in
the furrows of our world through the coöperation of God and
man together. On the other hand, there is most assuredly a type
of life presented in the Gospels which, when it appears, seems
to be already the Kingdom of God—a type of life in which love
is the supreme spring and motive, in which the spirit of forgiveness has come to ripeness, and which aims to do the will of God
on earth as it is done in heaven. In so far as the Church carries
on and incarnates that commission it becomes the sower of the
seeds of the Kingdom of God and the bearer of a new order for
human society.

There is a proverb which says that God empties the nest not
by breaking the eggs, but by hatching them. Not by the violent
method of revolution will the new social order of life come, not
by the legal enforcement of ancient commands, or by the formal
application of texts and sayings, but by the vital infusion of a
new spirit, the propagation of a passion of love like Christ's,
the continuation through the Church of the real presence of
Eternity in the midst of time will something come more like
the order of life which we love to call the Kingdom of God. It
is the rôle of the Church, I maintain, to be the fellow laborer
with God for this harvest of life. The true Church will be

proved to be the true Church, not by its legalistic conformity to the laws and practices of the first century, but by its spirit of love and service, its vision and insight of eternal realities, and its transmission of the Mind, the Spirit, and the Will of Christ here in the world of men.

The Church and the Present Social Order

By

ROBERT E. L. STRIDER, D.D.*

THE two most far-reaching questions a modern mind can ask
are: What are the functions of the state in the social order of
today? and What are the functions of the Church in the social
order of today? By the term "Church," as used in this question
and throughout this paper, is meant that religious organism
in all its manifold branches and subdivisions which claims spiritual allegiance to the person and work of Jesus Christ. The
pertinence of the first question to the safety and happiness of
man needs no argument. On every continent have arisen in our
day new governmental forms; new at least in method and
spirit; totalitarian in their reliance upon a single dominant
leader clothed with absolute political authority; totalitarian in
their demand that the whole of man—body, mind, immortal
soul—be dominated by the state; totalitarian in their claim to
be the final authority in all of man's allegiances; and totalitarian
also in subordinating truth, culture, science, even religion, to
the censorship of the secular power. The results of the emer-
gence of this totalitarian state can be seen grimly working themselves out in the countries of Europe, in Africa, in the Orient,
indeed in some measure in every land today.

On the other hand, the relevance of the second question we
have asked is possibly not so apparent. Nevertheless, a moment's
reflection should make clear that what happens in and to the
Church is of no less moment than what happens in and to the
state. The origins of both Church and state are to be traced into
the dim beginnings of the life of man. Now we see Church and
state arrayed in bitter warfare; now we see them proceeding
along parallel lines, ignoring each other; now, as in medieval
Europe, in close alliance, the Church dominating the state; now
we see them again allied, this time the state the more influential

---

* Protestant Episcopal Bishop of West Virginia.

partner; now we see them mutually dependent, respecting and supporting each other, as in a modern democracy; and now we see the totalitarian state supreme, the Church silenced and enslaved, where she is unwilling to be dictated to and controlled. Hence it appears that men are no nearer now to a final answer to the question, What are the functions of the Church in society? more particularly in relation to the state, than they were two or three thousand years ago. Yet many of us believe that a satisfactory answer to this question would go very far towards a solution of the problems which are vexing our souls today.

The most promising approach to such an answer to our question lies in a careful, open-minded consideration of the Christian Church in its relation to the social order, which accordingly is our subject.

I

To very many within and without the Church, the Church is not a social institution at all, but an agency for the comfort and delight of separate persons. Its task is to convert people one by one, to make them conscious of their sins, to bring them "to repentance and better minds," to baptize them, draw them into the wholesome fellowship of the Christian family, teach them to read their Bibles, attend Church, say their prayers, be good neighbors, and conform their daily lives to the principles enunciated in the Sermon on the Mount. The business of the Church is to comfort people in this world, and to prepare them for the joys of the world to come. As Dr. Charles Clayton Morrison says, in his unusually suggestive book, *The Social Gospel and the Christian Cultus* (page 183):

According to evangelicalism, the essence of Christianity is found in God's direct and unmediated dealings with the individual soul. Men are lost in sin and can be saved from sin to a life of holiness only by an inner regenerative act of God which takes place between God and the soul alone, through the mediation of Christ who is the soul's "personal savior." The inner life of the individual is the scene of that event which constitutes the unique and distinctive feature of Christianity. From this point of view evangelicalism reads the New Testament narratives and interprets the phenomena of the earliest days of Christianity, from Pentecost onward, as the preaching of this gospel of Christ as man's "personal savior" and the joyous and saving response of men and women to it.

But to others, while Christianity is assuredly a gospel for individuals, it is at the same time vastly more. Jesus was extremely solicitous for the souls of individuals, and He never, like so many lesser religious teachers, made the mistake of losing the individual in the mass. His evangelistic method was that of person-to-person witness and contact, as was illustrated in His choice of the twelve Apostles. He represented God as so interested in individuals that in His eyes men possessed infinite and precious worth. God loved men, and not just man. Nothing can happen to a human being, however humble or obscure, without the Heavenly Father knowing and caring. Even the angels in heaven rejoice when a sinner turning from his sin opens his heart to the love of God. No one has emphasized the value of each human personality as did Jesus of Nazareth. Indeed democracy, universal education, and social service, all stem directly from His teaching in this regard.

However, it is a grievous mistake to think of Christianity as a purely individualistic gospel. Notwithstanding what has just been said about Jesus' regard for the individual man, no one could have stressed the importance or sacredness of human relations more strongly than He. No one who was unkind, uncharitable, unforgiving, unwilling to help his fellow men, was fit to be His disciple. No man could enrich his own life by directly and selfishly striving to do so, but only by forgetting himself in the task of enriching the lives of others. To save one's life is ultimately to lose it. To be great is impossible save as one becomes a servant. To give one's life, to spend it freely without hope of reward, is the only unfailing recipe for happiness. These social emphases in the teaching and example of Jesus find their point and focus in His idea of the Kingdom of God.

The Kingdom of God was to Him a divine-human social order, not to be raised up in some infinitely far-off time, perhaps in the land beyond the grave, but already existing within the fellowship of those who had learned to call Him Lord. Jesus said that the Kingdom was in the midst of them, although its consummation could come only in the far-stretching future. Two points especially are to be noted: (1) The Kingdom of God is a social order, not a collection of unrelated individuals, although its beginnings are to be sought for in the personal lives of men and women. It includes all possible human relationships, as well as all human individuals, and would bring them into conformity with the rule of God. By no stretch of the imagination can Christianity be content to operate in the inner life of man alone, while his outer life, as expressed in contacts and relationships, goes untouched by its influence. The Gospel of Jesus visions a wholly redeemed social order, as well as wholly redeemed men and women. The present organization of society, as well as solitary persons, must be made obedient to the will and purpose of Almighty God. (2) The Kingdom of God is to be set up in the midst of the actual historical scene, not in some remote heavenly age. It is true that Jesus once said, "My kingdom is not of this world." It is a favorite text of those whose ways of life would be rudely disturbed by a fearless application of Christian principles to all departments of human activity. An industrialist of my acquaintance likes to quote it, when reminded that the Christian Church may properly have something to say with regard to the injustices and maladjustments of the capitalistic system. But clearly what Jesus meant was that His kingdom was not to be established through the use of worldly force. To say, "My Kingdom is not *of* this world" is not the same as to say, "My kingdom is not to be thought of as *in* this world." In the teaching of Jesus it is a commonplace that His disciples are always in the world, but never of it. The whole point about this aspect of the Kingdom of God is that it is a kingdom not of this world, but of God. It is here and now, in the midst of us, but it is of God. The most certain way to emasculate and nullify Jesus' idea of the Kingdom is to relegate it to some future age, or perhaps to the life beyond death. This is what the organized forces of evil in the world are ardently hoping for. For Jesus to have preached the coming of such a Kingdom would have meant to desert, not to save, the world. In other words, in the mind of our Lord the Kingdom of God was a social order, and the sphere of its operation was the historical scene of earthly existence. In like manner, the Hebrew ideal out of which the Christian gospel developed had to do with a social group. The Hebrew Church was the whole nation in all its corporate visions and acts. No one, then, can understand what it means for the Church to be a social institution, who does not remember that Judaism, the Lord Jesus, and the primitive Christians, all thought of religion as that which, while having its roots in the faith of the individual, goes on from there to create a society which shall reflect and reproduce the will of God. Social interest and emphasis are thus seen to be basic to the very nature of the Christian gospel. It is, therefore, meaningless to speak, as many do today, of a "social gospel" and a "personal gospel," as if Christianity were split into a dualism, and could be now one and now the other. There are not two gospels but one. Christianity is at one and the same time individual and social, and it is neither if it be not the other also.

The Church has sought throughout her history to be true to this vision of a redeemed society. It was so in the earliest centuries of the Christian era. Dr. Morrison on another page of the illuminating work already quoted (page 198) says:

It was the sense that they [the early Christians] were the heralds of a new order, and the accompanying consciousness of conflict between it and the existing world order, that aroused the emotions which issued in the new personal experience. In becoming Christians they were joining a revolutionary movement. They did not first have the personal experience and then the sense of social conflict. Their personal experience of saving fellowship with God and with one another was their inward reaction to the irreconcilable conflict which they felt to obtain between the coming Kingdom and the secular order of the world.

Following the period referred to in this quotation, the Church in the fourth century entered into an alliance with the state, accepting the leadership of the Emperor Constantine; and so began the magnificent medieval vision of a united Church and state, a divine-human theocracy on earth, which, however, after only a limited success as realized in the papal system, went to pieces on the rock of the Reformation in the sixteenth century.

Although Protestantism sought to reaffirm the personal and individual emphasis of Christianity, and succeeded in doing so to such an extent that, in the thought of many, Protestantism has come to be synonymous with rampant, undisciplined individualism, nevertheless not even Protestantism at its most pronounced has entirely lost the social ideal of the Christian religion. Dr. F. Ernest Johnson, in his book *The Church and Society* (page 97), quotes John Calvin on the social nature of Christianity. Says he:

In the Geneva of Calvin's day, the medieval principle of virtual identity between Church and community was carried out with magnificent consistency. For Calvin, "the gospel is not merely an energy which saves all the individuals who believe in it, it is not merely a comfort for individual burdened consciences, not merely the overcoming of errors which are dangerous to the soul, but it is at the same time the means of healing all public and universal ills, the element of purification and renewal for larger social groups, and the foundation-stone upon which this work of renewal must be based."

The Puritan ideal, both in England in the seventeenth century and in America then and later, was concerned with a Christian commonwealth in which the law of man and the law of God would coincide. Moreover, in the modern world, many extreme Protestant bodies are insistent upon the conversion not only of individuals but of society to the rule and mind of Christ. Thus the Protestant conception of the Church regards it both as a hospital for sick souls, and as a powerful leaven working to make the kingdoms of this world the Kingdom of God and of His Christ.

So far as the Roman Catholic Church is concerned, the same may be said, although that body would attain her end by different means. Some of the strongest expositions of the social implications of the gospel proclaimed in our day have been in encyclicals of different popes. Indeed some of these papal documents have been remarkable both for their grasp of moral and social principles, and for their clear vision of the trend of European affairs.

Thus both Protestantism and Roman Catholicism agree in declaring that the Christian Church, to be true to the vision and spirit of her divine-human Founder, without ceasing to minister to sick individual souls, must also be a social institution, never slackening her efforts towards the building of the Kingdom of God on earth.

II

This social ideal, then, growing out of the very nature of the Gospel, the Church in different ages and in various ways has sought to realize. She has not invariably been true to the spirit of her Head. She has suffered lapses in her social enthusiasms.

She has even at times allied herself with anti-social states, and become a means of human exploitation and oppression. Now and then she has shown herself to be quite indifferent to human suffering and woe. Sometimes she has promoted her own worldly prestige and enrichment at the expense of those she should have served. Nevertheless, in no period of her history has she entirely lacked prophetic voices to call her back to a vision of her social duty. To that call when clearly sounded she has more often proved obedient than recreant.

There are three ways in which the Church can function, and has functioned, as a social institution: (1) through the personal example and initiative of converted laymen and laywomen; (2) through organized groups within the membership of the different Church bodies; and (3) through the voice and influence of the Churches themselves, in their larger corporate capacity. We shall briefly discuss these in order.

As the individual Christian today looks out upon the contemporary scene, upon the forces of wrong, cruelty, and selfishness unleashed and wreaking their fury upon men and upon society, his reaction is apt to be a feeling of utter discouragement and futility. What can one man, one woman, any one individual, accomplish in the face of the mighty demonic forces rampant in the modern world? Human wisdom and ingenuity must inevitably reply, "Nothing whatever." And yet the history of Christianity reveals more than one instance of weak, isolated individuals, on fire with love of God and man, converted by the saving gospel of Christ, changing literally single-handed the course of history. These noble men and women realized the force of what one of the Oxford Conference reports says. (*The Church and Its Function in Society,* pages 189-190.)

Christian faith must express itself in the corporate life. There is no other sphere in which it can express itself. Christians, like other men, are members of society. They participate in the activities of the common life. The ways of serving God in the world are infinite in variety, but none are unrelated to the common life. To live is to act, and action is invariably conditioned in greater or less degree by the prevailing practice, customs, and institutions of society.

It is not surprising that in the face of the complexities of the corporate life Christians should be tempted to make a separation between the sphere of public action and the inner life of the soul. The corporate life appears to be dominated by forces that are irreconcilable with the Christian spirit of love. But to turn aside from the activities and struggles of common men is an evasion of Christian responsibility. The Christian is called to fulfill God's will, not in some remote and future world, but here and now in relation to the reality which encompasses, challenges, and resists us. Faith in God is real only as it confronts the particulars of history. Only by acting in accordance with God's will in the concrete historical situation in which He has placed us can we, in the full reality of our being, enter into fellowship with God. As Professor Brunner has written, retreat from the actual world would mean that "real action would be entirely withdrawn from the influence of the Christian ethic. It is *here*, in this borderland between technical action and ethics—in economics, in politics, in public life—that the great decisions are made. If the Christian ethic fails at this point, it fails all along the line."

It is possible that in the days of the Evangelical Movement in the Church of England, men contemplated the securely entrenched institution of slavery, and argued, from the fact that it had been an invariable accompaniment of civilization, and from the fact that commerce in England had been enormously enriched by it and fabulous fortunes made out of it, that therefore nobody could do anything about it, and that it would be best for nobody to try to do anything about it. Very likely tens of thousands of devout Christians salved their consciences with such arguments. But there arose a man, William Wilberforce, who, deeply converted through the evangelical preaching of the gospel and aided by others similarly converted, destroyed the baleful institution of human slavery so effectively that right-thinking persons ever since have regarded it as an evil not to be tolerated upon the face of the earth. Here was a far-reaching social reform brought about by the Christian Church largely through the heroic work and witness of one man.

In like manner a revolution in society's treatment of the criminal classes was started by a lone Englishwoman, Elizabeth Fry, because her Christian heart burned with compassion over the lot of countless wretches rotting in the jails and prisons of her time. A Christian woman, Florence Nightingale, went out to the Crimea to do what she might to relieve the sufferings of the soldiers, and who can estimate the value of all that has flowed, and until the end of time will flow, from her life and vision? Back in the last century, a heroic missionary to China was told that the door of that land was then locked, barred, and rusty on its hinges towards Christian missionary effort, and his unforgettable answer was, "Then let my life be oil for those rusty hinges." All that modern Christian missions have been able to accomplish in China began with that devoted Christian. William Carey goes to India, Albert Schweitzer to Africa, Wilfred Grenfall to Labrador, Peter Trimble Rowe to Alaska; a saintly Kagawa is raised up in Japan; a Jane Addams, a Lillian Wald, a Jacob A. Riis, labor for the poor, the dispossessed, the underprivileged in our congested cities; and a Father Damien works, lives, and dies in a remote colony of loathsome lepers. Yet men still ask in the face of the terrific social problems of the world, What can one man or woman do? The answer is that one Christian can do much, because the age of miracles is not past for those adventurous disciples whose hearts have been set on fire by the social urge, which is an essential element in the Gospel of Christ. Thus, it is through the lives and labors of choice individuals that the Christian Church in every age vindicates her right to be known as a worthy social institution.

The Church also translates her social message by means of organized societies and groups of lay-persons and clergy within the ranks of her constituents. Both the Roman Catholic and the Protestant Churches have in this manner made themselves felt as powerful social forces. The number of such societies in England is large, and their wholesome efforts notable. The Christian Social Movement in Great Britain began well back in the last century in the preaching and writing of F. D. Maurice and Charles Kingsley. This early impulse gave rise in 1877 to the pioneer socialist society of England, the Guild of Saint Matthew, associated with such names as Stewart Headlam, Thomas Hancock, Charles Marson, H. C. Shuttleworth, and Selwyn Image. The Christian Social Union began in 1889, the year in which *Lux Mundi* was published, and eventually included in its roster of members and leaders the names of Henry Scott Holland, Bishop Westcott, and Charles Gore. Social Service Unions in nonconformist Churches followed the Christian Social Union in the established Church. In time came the Catholic Social Guild and the Interdenominational Conference of Social Service Unions. These led on in due course in our day to the Conference on Christian Politics, Economics, and Citizenship, the famous "Copec," of which we have heard so much, and which is both nation-wide and interdenominational in scope and interest. Other Christian social movements in Great Britain are the Student Christian Movement, the Fellowship of Reconciliation, the Society of Socialist Christians, the League of the Kingdom of God, and Toc H, although the last is not organized along the same lines as the others mentioned.

In the United States, according to Maurice Reckitt, in his book, *Faith and Society* (page 190), "the birth of the Christian Social Movement may be dated from the founding of the Church Association for the Advancement of the Interests of Labor, in New York in 1887." In 1891, the Christian Social Union was organized in close affiliation with the parent society in England. The Church Socialist League dates from 1911, and out of it has come the Church League for Industrial Democracy. The Roman Catholic Church speaks in the United States on social matters through the National Catholic Welfare Council, and most of the Protestant Churches through the Social Service Commission of the Federal Council of Churches. The Protestant Episcopal Church functions socially through its National Department of Christian Social Relations.

From this bare enumeration it can be seen that the modern Church, both in Great Britain and in the United States, is alive to its social responsibilities. While these various groups do not and cannot speak on any issue in the name of an entire Church, they do reflect the social sentiments of very many, and their effectiveness is considerable, as research agencies and clearing houses for information and publicity. In some cases notable reforms have been brought about largely through the leadership of these groups, as, for example, the elimination of the twelve-hour day in the steel industry in 1920, and a distinct improvement in the moral tone of motion picture films, the latter greatly aided by a determined movement in the Roman Catholic Church. Whereas on the one hand, these socially minded groups cannot compromise or commit their Churches to any policy or movement whatsoever, yet on the other hand, in educating and arousing public opinion, they can be useful in ultimately bringing about reform. In fact a small group of determined persons who know what they want, and are firmly resolved to have what they want, can be much more aggressive and unified than a larger, more unwieldy body. Hence there are those who believe that the most effective way a Church can

fulfill its rôle as a social institution is not by seeking directly
and as a body to do so, but by encouraging and fostering small
groups of its members for purposes of independent agitation
and action.

A third way in which the Church can exert social influence
is through corporate action embodied in resolutions and pronouncements by councils, conventions, and other representative
assemblies. The Roman Catholic Church speaks as a great international Christian group through papal encyclicals, to which
reference has already been made. Such corporate action on the
part of Churches as a whole has its dangers. Sometimes resolutions by religious bodies are couched in terms so general that
no one can be certain what they mean. Again, resolutions may
not reflect the carefully considered opinion of the body as a
whole, but only of the small aggressive group which for special
reasons sponsors them, and for purposes of propaganda wishes
to avail itself of the prestige of the whole body. Yet again, resolutions are often innocuous, being popularly regarded as nothing
more than high-sounding, vague aspirations, having no "teeth"
in them, having behind them no adequate implementation,
and being in reality substitutes for action. Such pronouncements are rarely taken seriously, least of all by those entrenched,
privileged interests, individual and corporate, responsible for
the abuses against which the pronouncements are supposed to
be directed. On the other hand, carefully drawn resolutions
on social subjects, such as war and peace, industry, labor, politics, divorce, birth control, poverty, unemployment, and the
like, may not be entirely without value. They may serve at least
two important purposes.

(1) They are means for the moral and spiritual education of
clergy and laity, in an age when serious Christians are in sore
need of ethical guidance and support. Indeed, a special obligation rests on the Churches to give such guidance, because if
they will not, who will?

(2) Resolutions by representative Church bodies are an important factor in the creation and enlightenment of Christian
public opinion, and in democratic states public opinion is extremely important. Nothing could be more wholesome than
for people generally to cease thinking of the Christian religion
as a cloistered, dreamy system too flabby and spineless for the

organized forces of evil to fear, or even to regard as a foe, and to begin thinking of it as a virile, living, fighting force, cognizant of what goes on in the world, and determined to overthrow the kingdom of the devil in order to make way for the Kingdom of God. The great, materialistic, evil world does not take the Church seriously, because it considers that Christians do not mean business. It needs to be reminded that Christianity may be the most revolutionary, explosive, social force which can be introduced into the affairs of men. It probably was a shock to those in the ancient world who were compelled to give up their thought of the Gospel of Jesus as the impractical, harmless teaching of a starry-eyed visionary, and were forced to look upon it as so socially dangerous that its spokesmen could be described as "those who have turned the world upside down." A similar rude awakening may be in store for many in the world of our day.

It is thus that members of the Church must think of the gospel to which they are committed. Every one of us is under obligation to help make the Church the social force in history it was designed to be. In this connection may be quoted another paragraph from one of the Oxford Conference reports. (*The Church and Its Function in Society,* page 203.)

It is the members of the Church, who discharge the responsibilities of the common life in a countless variety of occupations and in an infinite multiplicity of daily acts and decisions, that are the leaven which leavens the whole lump. In this faithful, silent witness they are fulfilling the priestly function of the Church. They permeate with the spirit of Christian love the varied relations of men with one another and make them kindlier, humaner, and more wholesome. By their understanding of the true ends of life they unobtrusively criticize the standards of society and subtly change the attitude of their fellows. By performing their tasks in dependence on God and in the spirit of worship, they redeem the social life from the aridity and shallowness of secularism. These are what William James described as the "invisible molecular moral forces that work from individual to individual, stealing in through the crannies of the world like so many soft rootlets, or like the capillary oozing of water, and yet rending the hardest monuments of man's pride, if you give them time." [The quotation from William James is from *The Letters of William James,* vol. II, p. 90.]

III

It remains now to indicate in bare outline some of the basic principles by which the Church as a social institution must be guided, if she would attain her highest usefulness, and at the same time be true to her essential genius. These guiding principles are three in number.

(1) The Church as a social institution must be prepared to be a pioneer in ministering to the needs of men. One of the fixed points by which Jesus steered the ship of His work and teaching was human need. The world in His day was full of sorrow, poverty, pain, underprivilege, and misfortune. To Him these were as so many ravenous wolves gnawing at the vitals of the children of God, and in His eyes religion, which permitted itself to be insensitive to these needs, was a pitiful travesty of what religion is meant to be. Jesus would have said that faultless creeds, beautiful churches, dramatic services, and elaborate organizations, are utterly vain and empty, if compassion for suffering, exploited, hungry humanity go not along with them. He would have cried in the face of any Church, however loudly it might call upon His name, but which did not actually help people, that which Amos in the name of God centuries before had thundered in the ears of the Church in his day, "I hate your feasts and solemn assemblies." The Church must lead the way where human need appears. She may not without damage to her soul remain unmoved where men, women, and children are writhing under the scourge of wrong, injustice, or bitter fate. If there be a community which needs a hospital, a school, a home, or a child clinic, the Church is recreant to her trust and disloyal to the Man of Galilee, if she does not see that the needed institution is provided, either through a public campaign or by herself building and maintaining the institution. This is the justification for Christian social institutions on the mission field and in neglected areas at home. After public opinion has been aroused and the social conscience pricked awake, it will be no longer necessary for the Church to maintain such institutions; she can then withdraw so that the community or state can take over the work. But the point to be noted is that the public in such a case would not have become enlightened to the need,

and the need would not have been met, had not the Church led the way. In a backward community in West Virginia years ago the county authorities were unwilling to establish a public school. Accordingly the Church for many years, and at her own expense, maintained there a day school for upwards of one hundred children. Later the county school board came to see the light, assumed responsibility for the children of the region, and the Church closed her school. Thus twenty years of pioneer work was necessary to make a highly enlightened community aware of a crying social need.

This has gone on in tens of thousands of communities with like results. The Church alive to man's need has blazed the trail with hospitals, schools, and other social agencies, until at last the community, the state, or even the federal government, has come to see clearly that to which formerly it had been blind. It is because most communities these days are fully awake to the necessity of hospitalization that many think the day of the Church hospital is past. Possibly so, except for the maintenance of those already existing, and except in socially backward areas. Through her willingness, then, to be a pioneer wherever human need is manifest, a willingness which no Christian body may renounce, the Church deserves to be thought of as the greatest social institution in the world.

(2) The Church, if she would be a worthy social institution, must also recognize herself as a divinely appointed critic of all human systems and activities. She must never permit herself to be allied with anybody or anything so closely that she becomes embarrassed or hampered in the exercise of her function as a fearless and disinterested critic. The Church has a grievance against any force or influence which contravenes the fundamental truth of the gospel. The Church is at war with whatever in the modern world seeks to secularize, materialize, or dehumanize the life of man, whether it be the prevailing industrial system, the processes of popular education, or the state in any of its existing forms. It is for this reason that she must take an uncompromising stand against totalitarian governments, not because the Church is desirous of dictating what form of government nations shall live under. The Church can and will get along with any sort of civil government the nation may wish to set up, so long as her sacred principles are honored and upheld. It is untrue to say that the Church stands

or falls with democracy, or with any other form of government. She exists to redeem men, not to govern them. She is on the side of whatever ministers to that redemption. She is against whatever delays it, or makes it impossible.

Neither is the Church inextricably involved in the continuance of any particular social or economic order. Now and then we hear the remark that the Church has sold out to the capitalistic system. It is not so. Whatever economic order the Church is called on to live under she can and does coöperate with, but she reserves the right to be a fearless, and if need be a radical, critic of that order, the moment it begins to do violence to the letter or spirit of her gospel. And this applies to democracy and capitalism as it does to communism and national socialism. The Church has no program of civil government or of economics. She has a divinely revealed gospel. Therefore let government and economics be what they may, the demand of the Church is that they square with the truth of the eternal gospel.

How severely critical the Church has to be of much that is taken for granted as right and proper in the world of today, is suggested by the words of Professor R. H. Tawney. (Quoted in *The Church and Its Function in Society*, page 210.) Says Tawney:

Its emphasis [i.e., that of modern society] on the supreme importance of material riches; its worship of power; its idealization, not merely of particular property rights, but of property in general and as an absolute; its subordination of human beings to the exigencies, of an economic system; its erection of divisions within the human family based, not on differences of personal quality or social function, but on differences of income and economic circumstance—these qualities are closely related to the ends which capitalist societies hold to be all-important. In such societies, as the practice of the latter clearly shows, they are commonly regarded, not as vices, but as virtues. To the Christian they are vices more ruinous to the soul than most of the conventional forms of immorality.

(3) Lastly, the Church must take her stand well above the pettiness, the materiality, the selfishness, and the moral pessimism of the world, without fear or faltering, preaching her everlasting message as the only hope of man. Of course she must first set her own house in order. Otherwise she is not

worthy to proclaim her demanding and uncompromising gospel. The Church must be converted before she can hope to convert the world. In all her dealings, and in the personal dealings of her clergy and laity, she must exemplify the beauty and power inherent in her message, if she is to go forth to save society. The Church must never forget that she is not a human organization. She is a divine organism. And that fact gives her a lofty obligation to try to measure up to. In proportion as she does measure up to it, however, and in so far as her action and spirit convince the world that she is of heaven, not of earth, to precisely that degree will she be effective in reclaiming mankind for the love of God.

I can do no better in bringing this paper to a close than to quote the words of one of the greatest living Christian scholars, Professor Emil Brunner. (*The Divine Imperative,* pages 438-439.) His words are:

From this point of view her [the Church's] task of proclamation is not the development of a programme, or of individual points in a programme, but the awakening of the "social conscience," and the awakening of the conviction that to faith nothing is impossible. Above all she must herself confess the social guilt of Christendom, and must bow to the condemnation of the world as the condemnation of God. Through her proclamation of the growing Kingdom of God she must make strong and living the responsible will of Christian people for the creation of new and more righteous orders. As the one court of appeal, aware both of the order of Creation and of the order of Redemption, she must indicate what is in accordance with the orders of creation and of redemption, and she must claim every man for the demands of love. It is her duty to show the appalling contrast between the actual economic order and an economic order filled with the spirit of Jesus Christ, and it is her duty to proclaim the will of God as paramount even in the economic sphere. It is her duty to do this, without paying any attention to the opposition of politicians; she must also avoid becoming entangled with actual party politics. It is her duty, precisely because of the economic reality, to make the summons to Repentance: *Repent!* sound forth loudly and fearlessly; it is her duty to show that the evils in the economic sphere come from godlessness, and she must affirm that there is no other real improvement than that which comes through obedience to the Will of God. To use the phrase of Kierkegaard, she is called to proclaim the "absolute ideal," quite unconcerned as to whether it is "practicable" at the present time. In all this she is not to be concerned about economic and political possibilities; for in acting in this way she is indeed creating the possibility of a better economic order. Then, too, to lend still more weight to her message, she may point out how again and again the spirit of Jesus Christ has been the greatest force behind economic changes and transformations. In all this her message is very far from being an economic ethics. For her business is with the proclamation of the Kingdom of God, not with the ordering of the economic sphere.

I know of no finer statement of what we mean when we think of the Church in relation to the social order. Perhaps in days to come we, the Church's members and supporters, will be able to help her fulfill her high social function more nearly as her Founder and Head intended, when He sent her forth in all her weakness, but at the same time in all her glory, to preach His gospel to every creature.

The Rôle of the Church as a World Force

By

JOHN A. MACKAY, Litt.D., D.D., LL.D., L.H.D.*

The choice of the theme which the Bicentennial Committee has assigned to Bishop Tucker and myself is a reflection, I venture to believe, of a sentiment prevailing within this center of learning regarding the importance of religion and the Church. It has not been uncommon for universities in this country to acknowledge their debt to religion as the historic force that gave them birth. It has been much more uncommon for the emancipated institutional children of religious ancestry to take religion seriously as an important factor in the contemporary life of mankind. It is most uncommon of all for a great autonomous university to project into the program of a celebration, such as is now in progress on this campus, the significance of the Church as a world force. By doing this the University of Pennsylvania does more than pay tribute to the force, symbolized by the statue of George Whitfield, that brought it into being. It confesses its faith that the Christian Church as the great Mother still possesses the gift of parenthood and is relevant to issues, even to world issues, which are also the concern of a leading university.

I

No discussion regarding the Church should ever take place, especially in circles where the passion for clear thinking has its native seat, without the speaker making it perfectly clear in what sense the term "Church" is being used. For it has been truly remarked that "the question of the Church is the great unsolved problem of Protestant theology."

Sometimes the Church means the building where worship takes place. It may be "the little brown church in the vale" in the quiet of the wildwood, or a majestic cathedral like St.

* President, Princeton Theological Seminary.

Paul's in the heart of an afflicted metropolis. The Church may be the congregation which comes together for worship, in the open air or in some man-made sanctuary, simple or ornate, where the worshippers may be few in number or congregate in throngs to the services. The Church may signify one of the more than two hundred different denominations that make up the pattern of American Protestantism. Or the term may express a group of Church leaders representing many denominations who, from time to time, make pronouncements in the name of the Church, so that when they have spoken it may be said, with a certain amount of truth, that the Church has spoken. At times Church is used in general sociological terms as the institution in society which represents religion. Or the Church may be the sum total of all Christian communions throughout the world, the chief members of which, on the eve of the present titanic conflict, became united in the World Council of Churches at Utrecht in Holland.

Beyond and transcending these six meanings of the Church there is still another, the highest and holiest of all. The Church can also mean the great group of people, dead as well as living, belonging to every class and race and nationality, residing in every land and clime, members of all existing empirical churches and of none, who have believed in God through Jesus Christ and are members of the Body of Christ. This, and this alone, is the Church in the fullest Christian sense, the *una sancta*, the one holy catholic Church. As such the Church is at once wider and narrower than what we call the churches. It is narrower because large numbers who belong to the churches as we know them are not members of the Body of Christ; for their Christian profession, and so their Church membership, is of a purely conventional character. The Church in this sense is also wider than the churches that we know because many sincere Christians who live lives devoted to Christ have none the less, for one reason or another, never found a spiritual home in any of the existing churches. It is in the measure, however, in which the reality of the Holy Catholic Church is present in the churches that true churchly reality can be predicated of the latter.

In the present discussion we shall mean by the term "Church" the penultimate meaning in this series of seven. We shall think of it primarily, not as this or that Christian group, even should any one of the existing churches make exclusive claim to be *the* Church, but rather as the organized, corporate expression of all groups. In a word, Church, in this discussion, will really be the synonym of Christianity in its institutional aspect. We shall think of all Christian groups and their influence, from the Society of Friends to the hierarchial organizations, including such children of the Church as the Christian Associations and the Salvation Army.

II

Two main questions challenge our consideration. First, how far is it appropriate to speak of the Church in the above sense as a world force, actual or potential? Second, supposing this designation to be appropriate, what specific rôle should the Church play in order that its influence may be felt upon a world scale? Let us take up these two questions in order.

The first question can be answered very briefly. The major part of our discussion will center in the answer to the second.

World significance can be predicated of the Christian Church in a number of ways. (a) Universality is inherent in her nature and message. It is the Church's faith that God became man in Jesus Christ so that, in virtue of the incarnation, all human beings took on new meaning, and new possibilities of life opened up before mankind everywhere. The Church, as the prolongation of the incarnation, recognizes that her existence has no meaning unless all the people for whom Jesus died and rose again are made sharers in the spiritual benefits which God has bestowed upon men in and through Christ. The Church interprets her mission in the world as an expression of God's redemptive will to fellowship, namely, that the ultimate goal of history will be a society in which love shall be regnant in all personal relations, and loyalty to God shall be supreme.

(b) As the greatest single, institutional force in the life of some great powers which have world significance, the influence exerted by the Church within these nations constitutes, in a very real sense, a world force.

(c) World significance belongs also to the Church because it is today an ecumenical reality for the first time in history. This has come about through the unparalleled success of the Christian missionary movement during the last century and a quarter. The Christian Church in our time is literally a world society of a supra-national order. Organized groups of Christians are found in small numbers or in large in every representative area of the world. The Church is now coextensive with the inhabited globe. An ecumenical consciousness, moreover, has grown up in recent years among all branches of the Church through the holding of great world gatherings in which all branches of the Christian Church were represented. At the last of these gatherings, held in Madras, India, towards the close of 1938, more Christian groups were represented than at any previous time in the last two thousand years. These diverse Christian communions from the Occident and the Orient have discovered a remarkable unity.

The truth is that the Christian community has shown itself to be at the present time the most united, as well as the most universal, community in the world. In years when the international situation followed a tragic process of disintegration, the ecumenical situation became more and more consolidated. Whereas today the international problem consists in finding a common basis of understanding upon which nations may agree and coöperate, the ecumenical problem consists in applying the basic understanding already existing between Christians to all the problems of mankind. It is surely striking and providential that the ecumenical Church should have arrived at the very time when the world as a whole has become an ecumenical organism. When, for the first time in human affairs, physical unity and spiritual disunity can be predicated of the secular order in the most absolute sense, it is consoling that not since the Eastern Church separated from the Western, and the Protestant Churches left the Church of Rome, has unity been so real within the bounds of the Christian community. This ecumenical Church is a vast potential power.

We come, therefore, to the second question. Considering the Christian Church with its sense of world mission, its roots within great national groups, and its branches extending throughout the inhabited globe, what is its rôle as a world force?

The rôle of the Church is *to be the Church.* *"Let the Church be the Church."* This particular expression of the Church's function has been regarded as the most significant crystallization of thought that emerged out of the Oxford Ecumenical

Conference in 1937. The sentence in question appeared in the first draft of the report submitted to Commission V on "The Universal Church and the World of Nations." The sentiment and the phrasing were both adopted by the Archbishop of York's committee which drafted the Oxford Message. It has, since that time, been reëchoed around the world as a crusading slogan whose meaning is that the Christian Church should not be a servile imitator of other cultural or social groups, but should hold true to its own particular mission and nature. When the question is asked, When is the Church in very deed the Church? the answer is, when the Church bears witness to God whose organ it is for the coming of His Kingdom, His sovereign rule over the whole of life. Bearing this in mind, the way is open to formulate the principal phases of the Church's historic rôle in its witness to God as the organ of His redemptive purpose in human history.

III

When the Church is "in very deed the Church," she exercises a threefold function. The first function is *prophetic* in character.

For the discharge of her prophetic function the Christian Church possesses unique instruments to diagnose the condition of society and her own. The Bible, which among other things is the greatest treatise on human nature ever written, is part of the Church's heritage; the living Spirit of God abides in the Church; the Church knows by experience the reality of the transforming grace of Jesus Christ. That being so, the Church, when true to her nature, manifests insight into human situations and a sensitivity to human problems which cannot be paralleled by any other social group.

In the exercise of her prophetic function today certain insights are clarifying in the mind of the Church which she begins to proclaim in unequivocal terms. The Church recognizes that she, too, has "sinned and come short of the glory of God." Repentance therefore becomes her, for she has ofttimes been an unworthy witness to God. She is far from being guiltless for the present state of the world. When, therefore, the Church is confronted, as rarely before in history, with the unparalleled power of evil, and becomes conscious of her own impotence and ignorance, repentance, *metanoia*, as a complete reorientation of the mind and will towards God, has fresh meaning. For if the Church is to be a power as God's witness, she must think as God thinks and will what God wills.

Today, as in the time of the Hebrew prophets, Amos, Isaiah, and Jeremiah, the Christian Church in her ecumenical assemblies points men and nations to the fact that the divine order in the universe is violated by human sin and error. While not aligning herself with any political party or faction, or unfurling the banner of any social theory or group, the Church sets forth in the boldest relief her diagnosis of unhappy situations in which the welfare of men is being compromised and the principles of righteousness violated. The fact is emphasized that the universe has a grain, as timber has a grain, and that those artificers of human life are doomed who plane against the grain of the universe.

As the critic of all things human, the Church proclaims to the world of today, and to the democratic world in particular, that the failure of nations and of powerful groups within nations to regulate unregenerated economic forces has been responsible in great part for the present debacle of civilization. The Church's insight leads her to declare that the present crisis, in which psychopathic men and nations attempt to mold society after their monstrous likeness, is a direct consequence of the sins of Christian democratic powers. Their lack of sympathy and their positive cruelty prepared the way for the coming of totalitarianism. The Church proclaims also that no true world order can ever be established unless nations are willing to forego that which hitherto they have always insisted was the one thing they could not abandon, namely, national sovereignty. For if a nation insists that, at all times and under all circumstances, it shall continue to be sole and sovereign arbiter of its own rights and destinies, unwilling to submit to the will of any wider and duly constituted international tribunal, world order in any real sense will be impossible.

The nations must know, and the Church in our time takes means to inform their citizens, that the only possibility of having a stable and worthy political order is through God. John Middleton Murray has recently put the matter in the following striking form: "In order to recreate Caesar," he says, "we must rediscover God."

The most important attempt made by the Church to fulfill its prophetic rôle in recent times took place at the Oxford Conference in 1937. An increasing awareness that civilization was disintegrating led representatives of the Protestant and Orthodox Churches to meet together in order to think through the problems of contemporary civilization in the light of God and, if possible, to out-think the best thought in the world of to-day. A representative of the League of Nations who was present at that gathering remarked that not in all the long years he had served the League was he brought face to face with such a frank, unbiased, and at times brutal analysis of the true human situation.

This phase of the Church's prophetic rôle will be fully realized only when the Church succeeds, as she did in the past, in giving birth to an adequate theology. Starting from God's self-revelation, this theology shall take adequate account of the human situation and all human knowledge, and, in a massive and organized system, shall undertake the task which was undertaken at different times by Augustine, Thomas Aquinas, and John Calvin. The present rupture in civilization and the woeful compartmentalization of human knowledge demand once again the activity of unifying minds which are lit by the light of God and understand man and his world.

But if the Church, in the exercise of her prophetic gift, is to escape the stigma of exasperating the ills of today by pure moralism, and of offering mere ideals and panaceas to a world that is interested only in realities, she must listen afresh to the voice of God. She must proclaim in all its simplicity the redemptive evangel with full relevance to the situation of men everywhere. The Church affirms that the everlasting silence has been broken, that God Himself has spoken in such wise that there is a remedy in Jesus Christ for the evils which destroy human personality and human society. The Gospel entrusted to the Church is not a great imperative, but a great indicative. It does not consist primarily in a call to realize certain human ideals, but to accept certain divine realities. It does not invite men to achieve something; it invites them to receive something. It makes available for them new life which God Himself offers them, upon the basis of which they may build a new world.

In these last times a very special aspect of the Church's prophetic function has consisted in resisting every attempt on the part of secular powers to silence the Church's witness and make her the serf of some ideology or political system. There are parts of the world in which it is difficult for the Church either to exercise her prophetic gift, interpreting the human situation in the light of God, or to proclaim, with all its implications, the Gospel of God. All she can do in such a case is to bear witness to the fact that she belongs to God, that she is loyal to Him alone and refuses to accept any other loyalty. By doing so the Church offers a spiritual center of resistance to the overweening claims of the new secular churches, those totalitarian régimes that demand absolute allegiance on the part of citizens and provide for them in doctrine, fellowship, and worship, what the Christian Church is supposed to provide for her members. It was the noble resistance of the Confessional Church in Germany to the demands of the state at a time when great universities and learned societies succumbed before the mandate of the Fuehrer, that filled Albert Einstein and others with measureless admiration for the Church. Strangely enough, the stand taken by the Church in Germany and other lands in these grim days has exercised a greater and more world-wide influence on secular minds than many generations of preaching and theologizing.

IV

The Church has also a *regenerative* function to perform. Knowing by faith and by experience that God cares for the welfare of men, the Church devotes herself now, as in the past, to the transformation of human life in accordance with the pattern revealed in Christ. This involves making a contribution towards changing the conditions in which men live, and also towards changing human life itself.

It cannot be gainsaid, although sometimes it is but grudgingly admitted, that what is best in Western civilization has been the fruit of Christian influence mediated by the Church. Greece herself, it has been well remarked, was reborn to the world with a New Testament in her hand. Count Keyserling once observed that what was noblest and most truly human in the Russian experiment in its early days was the direct fruit of Christian influence.

Above all, democracy, especially in its Anglo-Saxon form,

which has been one of the most characteristic creations of Western civilization, is the child of the Christian Church. The foundations of democracy are built upon three great conceptions which the Church has inculcated: the majesty of truth as God-given; the worth of all men as creatures of God; and the reality of man's personal responsibility to serve God. Conviction regarding these truths led to important consequences. (a) Because truth is real and God-given, it is worth dying for. The fact that some men and some religious groups were willing to die for truth let the state, in the course of time, to decree religious toleration and liberty of thought for all citizens. (b) As men are of infinite worth in the sight of God, they should be treated with all consideration by their fellow men and be given every opportunity to fulfill their destiny as children of God. The affirmation of the worth of all men gave birth to the universal franchise. (c) Insistence by the Church that her members should take a personal part in the Church's work prepared men for citizenship and the service of society. As man is personally responsible to serve God, work was invested with a new dignity.

Now while it is true that Christianity existed before democracy and will continue to live on, in catacombs if necessary, whatever the fate of democracy may be, it is equally true that there are aspects of the Christian religion which cannot receive full expression save under the liberties granted by a régime which is either democratic or similar to it.

Not in all world history has there been a movement so decisive in its influence upon the secular life of mankind as the Christian missionary movement of the last century and a quarter. When the mists of the present have rolled away, and historians of tomorrow study calmly and dispassionately the history of modern missions within the context of the general history of civilization, it will be found that no influence ever made such an impact upon scores of nations in Asia, Africa, and Australasia, as that movement has done. In the trail of the Christian missionary and born of the Christian spirit came into being movements and institutions in the social, cultural, and political life of new peoples which have exercised a decisive, transforming influence upon their national life. As in this country, so also in many newborn nations around the world, how many of the best and most influential institutions have had a Christian origin! The Christian Church founded them; secular organizations carry them on.

The most outstanding example in the world of today of the creative work achieved in the life of a nation by the missions of the Christian Church is probably the Chinese Republic. While in China today, in the hour of the nation's crucifixion, there is only one Christian in every hundred, there is one Christian in six in the high places of government. It is this fact, as leading officials in the Chinese administration admit, that has given vision and patience to the Chinese spirit and endued the country as a whole with that magnificent resilience which has won the admiration of the world.

But the chief concern of the Church now as ever is not to transform the conditions in which men live, for that must largely be done by secular organizations inspired by the Christian spirit, but the regeneration of men themselves. If it is true that the strategist, as distinguished from the mere tactician, is the leader who never forgets the ultimate aim of the war, then the main objective in the strategy of the Church is not to provide questionable blueprints for a new order in Church or in state, but to bring all men to a first-hand experience of the living God. New men, Christian saints, are the Church's greatest need, as they are the greatest need of civilization.

It must ever be the Church's supreme task to create new men. Years ago at an international conference in Geneva I heard a professor of economics from the University of Lyons, France, make this remark: "It is not the function of the Christian Church to create a new civilization; it is the Church's function to create the creators of a new civilization." Who can measure the influence of the saints? It is not so much the great work accomplished by Toyohiko Kagawa in Japan that is of transcendent importance, but the quality of life which Kagawa has lived since student days in Kobe. That is what has inspired hundreds of thousands of people around the world. Similar in kind has been the influence of Albert Schweitzer, living the reality of Christian sainthood in his lonely vigil by an African river. But our modern saints must be of a new type. "Is it not high time," says Jacques Maritain, "that sanctity should descend from the heaven of cloistered life that four centuries of baroque spirit had reserved for it, descend to the world of secular culture and labor in social and political affairs with a view to the reform of the temporal order of mankind? Yes, indeed," he adds, "on condition that it retains its sanctity and does not lose its character on the way." The time has come for the Church to send some of her choicest sons and daughters, with the strength and fragrance of their sanctity, and with a burning, crusading passion in their hearts, into every sphere of the secular order.

V

Finally the Church has a *communal* function, that is to say, it is inherent in her nature and mission to establish the reality of true community. This she must do in the relations between people in each local Christian group, in the corporate relations of all Christian groups around the world, and, as far as possible, exercise a ministry of reconciliation in society as a whole. It is in this realm that the supreme contribution of the Christian Church must be made at the present time. For the Church, in accordance with the Oxford slogan, must be "in very deed the Church" that is, a fellowship of men and women who find within the Christian community a quality and strength of fellowship that cannot be found in any secular association. Now more than ever, amid the present breakdown of human relations, does the Church, as in the early Christian centuries, hold the world together. As the Church's full witness to God and His redemptive will to fellowship is made manifest and becomes more potent, a still greater and more effective unity will be witnessed among all Christians around the world.

We have happily reached a time when not only coöperation between different churches, but the organic union of many churches is taking place. Unity is a Christian duty, but the cultivation of spiritual unity, and the practice of effective coöperation on the part of Christians belonging to different denominations, do not mean that organic union ought to be entered into with precipitation. Care must ever be taken that union is not brought about for mere reasons of expediency, or because a sense of truth has been lost among those who pursue union. Where this happens the groups that become united bring no enrichment into the common life.

The next step in the ecumenical movement will, I trust, take the form of an effort on the part of each great Christian tradition to rediscover itself. This it must do by examining itself in the light of Holy Scripture, in the light of its own history, in the light of the testimony of other Christian traditions, and in the light of the challenge of the contemporary situation. In this way each will come to know itself and see clearly what there is in its own tradition that is merely ephemeral, and what there is in it that constitutes divine, imperishable truth. Thus will be avoided what is more to be dreaded than any other communal expression of Christianity, namely, a watery interdenomination-alism. If a union full of the strong wine of the Spirit is some-thing to be desired for its own sake, and because of the potent influence it will exert, nothing is to be more deprecated, and should with more tenacious insistence be avoided, than the watery fusion of strongly diluted church communities.

There presents itself to the Christian Church in these days a very tragic problem. War on a gigantic scale and for more abysmal stakes than at any previous time in the Christian era has rent the human family. It would appear as if the stage were being prepared for continent to be pitted against continent and not, as formerly, nation against nation. We have reason to thank God, as already stated, that before this tragic situation devel-oped branches of the Christian Church were planted in all the representative areas of the world. At this moment there are Christians on either side of the titanic conflict who pledged their troth to each other that, whatever happened in the polit-ical arena to divide the nations to which they owed allegiance, they would not suffer any situation to arise that would alienate their hearts from one another. The hope of civilization depends largely upon the loyalty with which those Christians are able or willing to carry out their pledge. If the Church holds together, as we believe it will, a new ethos, which is totally lacking in the world of today, will have fertile soil in which to develop. Out of that ethos will come a new spirit and a new world view.

Groups of Christians have been much concerned with the problem of the peace that shall follow the present war. All their thought, unfortunately, was based upon the assumption of an Allied victory. Now, alas, there is the grim possibility that even, if the totalitarian powers are not victorious, a cessation of hostilities from pure exhaustion or an armed peace at the end, may be expected. The question arises, how far will the Christian Church in such a situation be an effective force for peace and the restoration of comity? The situation is such that one "lifts up one's eyes unto the hills" and, in pure desperation, calls upon God for mercy upon our world.

This much, however, is certain: the supra-national can only be achieved through the supernatural. Even at the worst, should might conquer in these times, and send us back into new dark ages, new mission fields will be prepared for the activities of the Christian community. For the Church knows that in God's world might will not permanently triumph, she knows that Jesus Christ is Lord and that a will to fellowship, and not a will to power, shall ultimately prevail. To make that will prevail, the life and thought of the Christian Church are dedicated.

It is a time to live by hope. All our blueprints for a better world have been torn to shreds or filled with such blotches as to be scarcely recognizable. But there are things that cannot be shaken; the Church, the Body of Christ, remaineth.

The Rôle of the Church as a World Force

By

HENRY ST. GEORGE TUCKER, D.D., S.T.D., LL.D.*

THE inclusion of the subject dealt with in this paper in the program of the celebration of the two hundredth anniversary of the founding of a great university is a gratifying recognition of the fact that religion is one of the vital factors in the development of human society. If we may then assume that in every age religion has a part to play in promoting human welfare, it may not be inappropriate on this occasion to consider what during the past two hundred years the Christian Church has done towards the fulfillment of that obligation.

It would be impossible within the limits assigned to this paper to describe even in bare outline the Church's relationship to the social, moral, intellectual, and political development of the past two centuries. In some spheres of human activity the Church's rôle would seem to be much more limited today than it was two hundred years ago. In 1740, for example, education was in many Christian countries under the control of the Church. Since that time this responsibility has been gradually transferred from the Church to the State. There was a time when theology was spoken of as the queen of the sciences. During the period under review, however, the Church has not only relinquished its leadership in scientific advance, but not infrequently has taken its place on the opposition benches. Höffding in his *Philosophy of Religion* makes this comment on the changed rôle of the Church: "Christianity was once the pillar of fire, leading the human race forward in its march through history. It is fast becoming an ambulance lumbering along in the rear, picking up the dead and wounded."

This pronouncement of Höffding's, like most epigrammatic general statements, is far too sweeping to be an accurate description of the part played by Christianity in efforts to promote human well-being during the past two hundred years. Organized

---

* Presiding Bishop, Protestant Episcopal Church.

Christianity has not infrequently adopted a very conservative attitude towards proposals for reform. On the other hand, such reforms have in a great number of cases been inaugurated and carried through to effective operation by individuals and groups who derived their inspiration from the Christian religion. A striking illustration of this is the leadership furnished by the Friends and Evangelicals in England in the successful attempts to abolish slavery and to bring about prison reform. Another more recent example is the strong protest made by leaders of the Roman Catholic Church against morally degrading moving pictures.

While one might cite many other examples of the contributions made by Christianity to human welfare, yet there has been an undoubted tendency to seek the solution of major problems independently of any aid from religion. This tendency began as an effort to win freedom from the too rigid ecclesiastical dominance in all spheres of thought and practical endeavor that had been established during the Middle Ages. It was not in the beginning an attempt to drive religion out of life. On the contrary, it owed its early momentum largely to the demand for freedom in religion. Gradually, however, the assertion of the right of private judgment developed into the conviction that the human reason was competent to discover truth without the help of revealed religion. Along with this grew the assumption that the truth so discovered could be applied to the solution of practical problems through the use of human capacities.

This doctrine of human competency was tremendously reinforced by the progress achieved during the nineteenth century through the application of scientific principles to various spheres of practical endeavor. We entered the twentieth century with a widely spread feeling of optimism. Much still remained to be done, but mankind was fairly confident of its ability to establish through its own efforts a human society in which would be realized all the blessings of the Christian conception of the Kingdom of God upon earth.

What, we may ask, was the effect of this process of secularization upon religion? It has not resulted in any widespread repudiation of religion as such. It has, however, gravely affected the rôle of religion, and at times it has so sapped its vitality as to incapacitate it from performing its proper functions. At

the time, for example, when this University was founded, religion in England was at a low ebb. This was due to a combination of causes, but one of the most potent of these was a
widely spread rationalism, which might be described as belief
in the competency of human reason. Theologically this philosophy expressed itself as Deism. The existence of God was not
only granted but strongly affirmed. Voltaire is reported as saying, "If there were no God, it would be necessary to invent
one." What was repudiated was man's dependence upon God
in the conduct of his earthly affairs. Mr. Chamberlain once characterized the attitude of the Japanese towards religion as a
"politeness towards possibilities." The practical relationship of
the Deist towards God might be expressed in somewhat similar terms. A story is told of a French ruler, who was not noted
for devotion in religion, tipping his hat as he passed a church.
In reply to someone who expressed surprise at his showing such
reverence to God, the ruler replied, "We salute, but we do not
speak."

Deism took away from the Christian Gospel just those elements which led St. Paul to affirm that it was the power of
God unto salvation. While it did not repudiate Christian morality in theory, it reduced the Church's efficiency in performing its rôle of promoting it almost to the zero point. It viewed
with contempt any approach to enthusiasm in religion. The
resulting conditions illustrate the truth of what the author
of *Ecce Homo* had in mind when he declared, "No heart is
pure that is not passionate; no virtue is safe that is not en-
thusiastic."

The corrective to this lamentable state into which English
religion had fallen was supplied by the Evangelical movement
inaugurated by Wesley. Socrates was said to have found philosophy in the clouds and to have brought it down into the
streets. In like manner, Wesley strove to bring back God from
the remote position to which He had been relegated in the
Deistic interpretation, into the lives of individual men and
women. The results of this revival of the religious life of
England were manifested in social and moral reforms in the
home country and also in the creation of a feeling of responsibility for the spiritual and moral welfare of the non-Christian
world.

The emphasis of the Evangelical movement was upon con-

version and personal religion. Its theology was of the type that
in our time is called Fundamentalism. It showed no particular
interest in the idea of the Church, or in corporate worship.
While it was perhaps well suited to meet the religious needs of
an age which thought of society as an aggregation of individuals, it was unable to adjust itself to the transfer of emphasis
from the individual to the social whole which took place in the
nineteenth century. Professor McMurray once said the eighteenth-century concept of society might be represented by the
formula, one plus one equals two, while in the nineteenth
century this conception was replaced by that of the biological
organism. Within the Church of England the growing dissatis-
faction with the indifference of the Evangelicals to the value
of corporate whole gave rise to the Oxford Movement. We are
not concerned in this paper with the purely ecclesiastical developments that resulted from this movement. It is pertinent,
however, to note the interest displayed by many of its ad-
herents in social problems. One practical manifestation of this
interest was a widespread effort for betterment of conditions
in the slums of London and other large cities. This represented
an extension of the rôle of the Church to an area which had
previously been grossly neglected.

While the Oxford Movement represented an adjustment to
changed ecclesiastical conceptions, and the increased interest
in social problems and in foreign missions indicated that in the
sphere of practical endeavor the Church was heeding the signs
of the times, the situation was quite different with regard to
the changes in the world of thought.

One meaning of the doctrine of the Holy Spirit is that the
Church is competent to steer its course steadily and safely between the Scylla and Charybdis of continuity and change. This
principle is clearly asserted in the Preface to the Book of Common Prayer with regard to forms of worship. "It is but reasonable that upon weighty and important considerations, according
to the various exigency of times and occasions, such changes
and alterations should be made therein, as—from time to time,
seem either necessary or expedient." The guiding principle in
making such changes is quaintly described as "seeking to keep
the happy mean between too much stiffness in refusing, and
too much easiness in admitting variations in things once advisedly established." A study of the history of such changes

shows that they were due not only to changes of customs and manners in the Christian community itself, but also to the incorporation or baptism into Christ of practices and forms which were originally not Christian. Even today in the Orient we see the same process going on to some extent.

The Preface to the Prayer Book does not, however, indicate that the same principle might legitimately be followed in the development of Christian theology. In that sphere the test of orthodoxy is "that which has been accepted always, everywhere, by everybody." The faith once for all delivered to the saints must be preserved unchanged as a sacred trust. These are perfectly valid principles in so far as they are interpreted as meaning that in religion, as in life, change must be consistent with the preservation of continuity. St. Paul calls Christ the new Adam, that is, He was the progenitor of a new type of man spiritually. Christ Himself insists that we must be born anew. St. Paul describes a Christian as a new man in Christ Jesus. This type must be preserved. Any change which transformed us into new men in someone else would be illegitimate. On the other hand, the drawing out of all the implications of the new man in Christ Jesus is a long process. Any change which makes actual the potentialities of this new man is not only legitimate, but one may even say obligatory, or at least essential for continual well-being.

The same principle applies to Christian truth. It begins with what was given through Christ. That determines once for all the type, if we may call it so, of Christian theology. We cannot substitute a different idea of God for that revealed to us through Christ. Our relationship to God must always be that which Christ established in His life, death, resurrection, and gift of the Holy Spirit. He is the same, yesterday, today, and forever. But our apprehension of the full meaning of this revelation must develop. Christ said that one of the functions of the Spirit was to lead us into all the truth. All truth, wherever encountered and whenever discovered, must be baptized into Christ in the firm conviction that it will enrich our understanding of the full meaning and the proper application of the truth revealed through Him. In this process of incorporation we must be guided by the Holy Spirit, lest haply our efforts result in the substitution of a different type of truth rather than the development of that which was derived from Christ.

The Nicene Creed is an illustration of the application of this principle by the Church. Christianity came face to face with Greek thought. Instead of looking upon it as something entirely alien from the truth as it is in Christ Jesus, it strove to baptize it into Christ with the result that our understanding of the faith once delivered to the saints was greatly enriched.

There is doubtless danger in this effort to incorporate the truth which we encounter into Christian theology. This danger was perhaps not altogether avoided by those early theologians who attempted to baptize into Christ Greek philosophy and Roman legal conceptions. Anselm created tremendous problems for future theologians by attempting to use certain feudal principles in working out his doctrine of the Atonement. While, however, this danger must be kept in mind, this is a task which the Church must be prepared to undertake whenever it comes face to face with what claims to be a discovery of new truth. Gamaliel expressed the correct attitude towards new truth when he advised the Jews to refrain from persecuting Peter and John: "If this counsel or this work be of men, it will come to naught, but if it be of God, ye cannot overthrow it; lest haply ye be found even to fight against God." Every alleged discovery of new truth needs to be investigated. It may be incompatible with Christian truth, but it may be material which God is offering and which, if used under the guidance of the Holy Spirit, may enrich theology and increase its value in helping us solve the problems of our age.

Unfortunately, the Church was unprepared to act on this principle in dealing with the revolution in the world of thought caused by the scientific developments of the nineteenth century. The Darwinian hypothesis of evolution, for example, was judged by most Church leaders to be utterly incompatible with the Christian doctrines of God and of His relationship with the world. Many of the leaders of science acquiesced in this judgment and proceeded to devise an interpretation of the universe from which God was excluded as a vital factor. While this philosophy of naturalism did not win wide acceptance among the masses of the people, yet the application of scientific discoveries to the problems of life was so productive of results that it was followed in practice even by those who rejected it in theory. In the sphere of practical endeavor, science displaced religion as the "pillar of fire leading the human race

forward in its march through history." In other words, the
principle of the separation of Church and State was extended
to all departments of human activity. The area in which man's
dependence upon God was recognized shrank to very small
dimensions.

This antagonism between science and Christianity in the
realm of thought affected adversely their respective rôles in contributing to the advancement of human well-being. Science is
concerned with process rather than with values. It showed men
how natural resources could be used for the accomplishment
of results. Its primary function was to show the method by
which ends could be attained. The question what ends should
be sought was outside of the scope of its responsibility.

This does not mean that scientists were indifferent in regard
to moral values. They accepted the standards of conduct that
had been developed under the guidance of the Christian religion. Even those who repudiated the doctrines of Christianity
for the most part sincerely desired to retain its moral code.
They would doubtless have agreed with John Stuart Mill, who
said that in determining his moral conduct a man could do no
better than to follow the example of Jesus Christ. Like Mill,
however, they did not consider that the Christian belief in
God was necessary for the maintenance of these standards. If
they made for human happiness, rational man in an age of enlightenment could be safely trusted to conform to them. This
optimistic estimate of man's moral competency made them
oblivious to the danger of placing great power in his hands.
Huxley, indeed, was pessimistic as to the moral outcome of
man's struggle with a nature whose trends were irrevocably
evil. While, however, the fact that nature was red in tooth and
claw made belief in a good God difficult for many, yet there
was a naïve confidence that the evolutionary process was headed
towards the good. It was, perhaps, natural to assume that the
general betterment which man was effecting through the aid
of science would include moral progress.

The events of the past twenty-five years have forced us to
perceive the fallacy of this assumption. We see in our time
not only individuals, but whole nations using the tremendous
power which science has enabled them to develop, for ends
which are the very antithesis of those advocated by the scientific pioneers of the nineteenth century. In pursuing this course

they are not conscious of violating moral standards. On the contrary, they have deliberately repudiated some of the basic principles of Christian morality and substituted others which, from the point of view of the philosophy they have come to accept, that is to say of their basic beliefs, seem more reasonable. It should also be observed that those people whose moral ideals have thus been brought into conformity with their fundamental convictions develop remarkable energy in acting upon them. On the other hand, those who still retain the moral convictions which were originally derived from the Christian religion, but whose philosophy of life has been formed from other sources, frequently are incapable of generating the power which is essential for the realization of moral aims.

Are we not, then, led to the conclusion that the once familiar saying, "It makes no difference what a man believes, provided only he lives a good life," is utterly fallacious? Our belief represents the judgment which we pronounce upon the nature of the situation in which we are placed. Having pronounced that judgment, we determine how we should act in view of the situation. This is what we call rational conduct. If our situation includes only the physical universe, and we refuse to take into consideration God and what we may call the spiritual realm, morality based upon religious conceptions will sooner or later be adjudged irrational. It is not the kind of conduct that our situation calls for.

Is not this the position in which many people today find themselves? Theoretically they still retain their religious beliefs. They acknowledge their obligation to conform to the moral standards which follow traditionally from these beliefs. In their secular activities, however, their judgment as to what is rational and valuable is determined by an entirely different philosophy of life, one in which faith in God plays but little part. It is not strange, therefore, that the moral ideals which they derive from their religion are often looked upon as counsels of perfection, which are impracticable under the conditions that prevail in what seems to them the real world. Kant's doctrine that "ought" implies "can" is true only when our conceptions of obligation and practicability are derived from the same source. The difficulty of the present situation is that our "oughts" come to us from the Christian faith in God as a real factor in life, while our "cans" are determined by the philosophy of human competency. The disciples on one occasion were so astonished at an idealistic pronouncement of Christ's that they exclaimed, "Who then can be saved?" Christ replied, "The impossible things of man are possible with God." Experience shows only too clearly that if we leave out God, our "oughts" will inevitably be reduced to what we conceive to be practicable within the limits of our human capacity. As the old English proverb puts it, "A bird in the hand is worth two in the bush."

If these considerations have any validity, they have a very pertinent bearing upon the subject of this paper, the rôle of the Church. The rôle assigned to the Church by its founder was the establishment of the Kingdom of God upon earth. The Kingdom of God on earth means the conformity of all human activities, both individual and corporate, with the will of God as revealed to us by Christ. We attempt to give practical expression to this will of God in what we call Christian moral standards. We might say, then, that the rôle of the Church is to proclaim these standards and to invite men to conform to them. In other words, the Church's function is to give moral guidance and leadership to the world. In this attempt, religion is used as a valuable means of arousing men's emotions in support of the Christian program. Matthew Arnold has described religion as "morality touched with emotion."

This conception of the Church's rôle makes religion a means and morality an end. There are, however, two fatal objections to such a conception of the relationship between religion and morality. First, it is impossible to win genuine acceptance for a Christian program from men whose sense of values is derived from a non-religious interpretation of the world they live and work in. Second, such a program is incapable of being maintained by our human capacities working apart from God. "Without faith," says the Bible, "it is impossible to please Him." If the past one hundred years teach us any one lesson, it is the truth of that statement. When Nicodemus came to Jesus to inquire about His teaching, Christ's reply was, "Except a man be born again, he cannot see the Kingdom of God. That which is born of the flesh is flesh, and that which is born of the Spirit is spirit." "The natural man," says St. Paul, "receiveth not the things of the Spirit of God: for they are foolishness unto him." Experience again confirms the truth of these words. It is unreasonable to expect the natural man, the man whose values have been derived from the philosophy of naturalism and whose capacities are those which physical nature supplies, to accept and carry out a program such as that outlined in the Sermon on the Mount.

Our conclusion, then, is that the prime function of the Church is to promote and foster faith in God. The Kingdom of God is not simply a program presented to us for our consideration and adoption. It does, indeed, contain a program, but it is one in which the chief part is played by God Himself. Christ commanded His disciples to go into all the world and preach the Gospel. St. Paul defines the Gospel as the power of God unto salvation. This power that comes to us through faith in God is not a substitute for physical power. Thanks to science, we are already in possession of ample physical power and we have learned how to use that power for the promotion of physical well-being. There is prospect of still further advance along both these lines. So far as physical power is concerned, if we were determined to follow the Communist principle of every man producing according to his ability, the amount of possible production would doubtless be sufficient to carry out the second part of their principle, every man to receive according to his need. There are two reasons, however, why this is not an adequate formula for the attainment of human well-being. In the first place, both on the producing and the receiving side, man lacks the moral qualifications which are essential for its successful operation. The second fallacy is the assumption that human well-being would be assured by the satisfaction of man's physical needs. There is in man a spiritual hunger which nothing that is of the earth earthy can assuage. He may not, indeed, be conscious of it, but it is none the less destructive of his happiness. Lack of appetite is as dangerous a symptom in the spiritual sphere as in the physical. "Blessed," says Christ, "are they that hunger and thirst after righteousness: for they shall be filled." From ancient times there have been those who recognized this need and also the fact that God alone can satisfy it. "As the hart panteth after the water brooks, so panteth my heart for thee, O God." "Man shall not live by bread alone, but by every word that proceedeth out of the mouth of God." "My soul was made for thee, O God, and cannot find rest until it rest in thee," said St. Augustine.

When St. Paul calls the Gospel the power of God unto salvation, he means a power that will provide these two prerequisites for human well-being. Where they are lacking, physical power in the long run proves to be a power for destruction rather than for salvation. This has been so abundantly illustrated in recent experience that there is today a widespread tendency to recognize this need that has for a long time been neglected.

This affords an opportunity, even a challenge to the Church to concentrate its efforts upon the performance of its primary function, bearing witness through its own life to the saving power of God. "God was in Christ," says St. Paul, "reconciling the world unto himself . . . and hath committed unto us the word [or the ministry] of reconciliation." Much might be written as to the details of the program of activities that is implicit in St. Paul's statement of the rôle of the Church. This program, however, is utterly without significance, except in so far as the power of God operates in it and through it. The subject assigned for this paper is "The Rôle of the Church as a World Force." The only justification for calling the Christian Church a force in world affairs is that it is the agency through which the saving power of God is brought to bear upon the world's activities. The marching orders given to it by its Founder and chief Captain were, "Go ye into all the world, and preach the gospel to every creature." As it goes forth to carry out this command, its marching song is:

> Christ for the world we sing
> The world to Christ we bring . . .

How Christian-Jewish Ideas Affect Christian-Jewish Conduct

By

MORRIS S. LAZARON, Litt.D.*

THAT men should differ with each other in their views of life is but natural. These differences extend over every area of thinking and conduct. Men have fought about politics and possessions, over liberties and laws, since that dim dawn when the emerging personality vaguely recognized its own worth, rights, and dignity. No wonder, then, that men have differed and fought about religion, because religion emphasizes man's dignity in his own eyes as a child of God.

Struggles in the realm of religion, however, reveal an irony in things that repels the sincere, confirms the doubter, and despairs the hopeful. That people who say they believe in God, Who is Father, and that all men are brothers, should hurt and hate each other is tragic irony in the cosmic manner. We can at least derive some comfort from the contemplation of how deep and sincere man's convictions can be, and we can mutely wonder at the power convictions give to conduct.

We might paraphrase Goldsmith's familiar lines: And still we gazed and still the wonder grew, that man's small head can stir up such a stew.

We have not the time to survey Christian-Jewish relations historically. The general outlines of the Christian-Jewish tragedy are familiar, and contemporary events are insistent. Suffice it to say that many factors which are not at all religious, either in idea or implication, play a part. Differences of belief and the theologies man created to express them were considered fundamental, but the historian and the psychologist will also point with truth to considerations of economics and politics, and the vicious circle of thrust and counterthrust, of attack

---

* Rabbi of the Baltimore Hebrew Congregation.

and defense, to the confidence which victory gives, and the compensations which defeat evokes, as powerful influences in the tragic drama of man's search for God and the good society. One item will illustrate the point.

Professor Arthur Ruppin, distinguished sociologist at the Hebrew University in Jerusalem, in his book just published, *Jewish Fate and Future*, refers to these collateral factors. He declares:

The migrations of the Jews in the Diaspora are distinguished from the early mass migrations of other peoples by the fact that the Jews did not march into new territory in serried ranks and militarily occupy it, but arrived singly or in small groups and had no force with which to conquer for themselves land already held by other races. Thus they had no conquered soil to farm; and as non-members of the autochthonous tribes they could not acquire land by purchase: the land was, indeed, usually tribal property. The Jews thus remained landless. And as status within the community depended on ownership of land, the original inhabitants looked upon the Jews as aliens, a circumstance which has operated against the Jews down to our own day, finding recent expression in the Nazi anti-Semitic catch-phrase, "blood and soil."

A religion should not be judged only by the universality of its idea. Any concept of the infinite God must have as corollary the concept of human brotherhood. Rather the genius and test of a religion ought to be measured by how it applies the universal idea. I say I believe in one God who is Father, all men are my brothers, and Israel is the Messiah people, the priest people, humanity's teacher; or I say I believe in one God, the Father, and Jesus Christ, His Son, my Redeemer and Saviour, in the grace and power of the Holy Spirit, and God's plan of redemption through Christ Jesus. Very well. But how do these beliefs express themselves in my personal relations with those who believe otherwise? How do they manifest themselves in the conduct of the organized synagogue or church in its relations with other organized religions? That is the test.

The Psalmist said, "Out of the mouth of babes and sucklings cometh wisdom." Some time ago I received a letter from a Christian youth who told me his best friend was a Christian Scientist. They often argued religion. "I think I am right, and he thinks he is right. But I suppose," he wrote, "that what really counts is what sort of a fellow my religion makes me."

One hard question organized religion faces today is the recognition of three apparently contradictory concepts: its idea of universality, its claims to authority, its respect for the sanctity of differing human personalities. It is in this area that tension and conflict arise within and among Christian and Jewish groups.

The problem is recognized and attempts are made to meet it. Not infrequently we hear something like this: that we must distinguish between intolerance of the idea and intolerance of the person; we must be intolerant of the idea, but we must always be tolerant of the person. This is hardly helpful, as history proves. It is only a short step from intolerance of the idea to intolerance of the person who holds the idea; and logic and practicality combine with psychology to hasten the procedure from idea to person. I don't like the idea that John espouses. I believe it is not only fallacious but wicked. I combat the idea; but John remains incorrigible. This irritates me, so I turn my batteries from John's idea to John himself. Pity poor John, if I have enough political, economic, or police power to put him under pressure of my convictions.

The meat of the matter is the question of authority. In a real sense, what is taking place today is another chapter in the story of man's quest for authority. We are so framed that we need to yield loyalty to some law, both as individuals and as nations. Because of this need, man created the systems under which he lives; in his quest for authority, he evolved political forms, economic organizations, and religious patterns. Ever and again came periods when authority was destroyed, stability lost, and certainty fled. These were periods of revolution. Such is the character of our times.

It was much easier for St. Thomas to attempt harmonization of all the knowledge of his day, and with a measure of success—though the success be only in the creation of a schematism—than it is for men of our time. The attempt of the neo-Thomists to cut the pattern for twentieth-century thinking and conduct to Aquinas' thirteenth-century model is certainly a brave and interesting effort; and though there are and always will be millions who find authority in religion a source of healing and strength, there are other minds who will not yield their freedom, and for whom the authoritarian atmosphere and discipline are as uncongenial in the sphere of re-

ligion as in the spheres of economics and politics. This is a
fruitful field for friction. Ideas do not exist in vacuo. Protestants, Catholics, and Jews naturally *act* about contemporary
events as they are taught to believe and do believe about them.
The question then becomes: How do Catholic, Protestant, and
Jewish belief influence Catholic, Protestant, and Jewish conduct? How does official sectarian religious opinion, backed by
religious organization, influence public action? How does Protestant, Catholic, or Jewish belief influence action in relation
to Communism, Fascism, Nazism; in attitudes toward Russia,
Germany, Italy, Poland, Palestine, Spain, Ethiopia, Mexico,
Quebec Province, and the South American Republics; in relation to the problems of education and social controls within
the nation? These particular matters will probably be dealt
with by my comrades on this program. Therefore it is sufficient
to point out the inevitable relation between idea and action,
between belief and practice.

It might be urged that there is no unanimity within the
groups. That is true. Not all Catholics think or act alike. Nor
do all Jews and all Protestants. But there is a direction to thinking, backed by the authority of tradition and often by the authority of organization, which it is difficult for individuals to
ignore.

I believe we must frankly face the fact that conflict between
religions in the area of authority, where religious conviction
flows over into social, political, and economic action, is normal.
But frictions arise also from the very claims to finality and authority which the religions themselves make. I can understand
you when you tell me, "I have the truth." I may not believe
that truth of yours. I may reject it, but I can understand it.
Here is the key to better relations in the area of authority:
The recognition of the possibility of my yielding allegiance
to authority other than yours. For religious liberals the problem presents itself in still another form. Is there no other alternative than the authority which revealed religion claims for
itself? The question is significant, because there are those who
say that with the apparent breakdown of faith and religion, as
of economics and international relations, there is no alterative
but to move forward to some sort of religious authoritarianism.

I believe there is an alternative authority; an authority which
has been won through sacrifice and the blood of martyrs. It is

the authority of the free human spirit in an autonomous moral order. This authority of the liberated yet disciplined mind has wrested from all the tyrants of the past new areas of achievement, has opened new and larger horizons, has broken many shackles and set slaves free. It has given man a sense of indignation at wrong, has fortified his will to make right that which is wrong. It has deepened his sense of social obligation. It has glorified his instinct for compassion. At times of emergency, it has voluntarily relinquished its prerogatives and pooled its powers for the general good. It has been expressed in the political, economic, and religious organizations of the world. Its free expression has modified some of those organizations, discarded others, and created new ones.

The authority of this disciplined yet liberated mind of man must be increasingly expressed in the politics, economics, and religion of today. No dictatorship of individual or party, or group or nation or race, or even of religion, can supplant the authority of the free mind. It is autonomous. It does not derive from force ruthlessly used or from ignorance willfully imposed. It derives from God. An increasing respect for this interpretation of authority will be an essential factor in bettering Christian-Jewish relations. Translated into practical terms it means fair play, it means refusing to take advantage where number or influence makes advantage possible. I believe we are making headway in this field.

We have been dealing up to now with the inescapable differences of religious philosophy which lead to tension and conflict between religions. There are, however, great affirmations which Jews and Catholics and Protestants share together. These affirmations are: belief in God, in a personal God, in the spiritual interpretation of life and the universe, in the ethical implications of religion. These affirmations flow over into social ideals shared by Christians and Jews, because they are rooted in the Judaeo-Christian tradition. Today they are challenged as ideas; they are attacked and flouted as ideals of conduct.

A few days ago, one of the great intellects of the world summoned religion to abandon the "concept of a personal God," and declared:

In their struggle for the ethical good, teachers of religion must have the stature to give up the doctrine of a personal God, that is, give up that source of fear and hope which in the past placed such vast power in the hands of priests. In their labors they will have to avail themselves of those forces which are capable of cultivating the good, the true, and the beautiful in humanity itself. That is, to be sure, a more difficult, but an incomparably more worthy task.

This is an old conflict, and probably our children's children will be arguing it long after the vibrations of our voices have reached the ends of space. Certainly the authority of this great scientist and the integrity of his character command respectful attention for anything he says. It may be that his point of view prefers to certain theological ideas which he has broadened mistakenly to cover the entire field of religion; or it may be that he who wrote a widely read paper some few years ago in which he proclaimed his faith in the God of the Psalmists, of Assisi, and Spinoza is not so far from the inner shrine, after all.

At any rate, one simple believer, in all reverence for the towering intelligence of the master, suggests the possibility that to hold to the idea of a personal God requires also certain qualities of spirit equal in stature to those which relinquishment of the idea might demand; and, furthermore, that to proclaim and to try to live such belief is a difficult task and one of incomparable worth.

Like doctors and religionists, perhaps because they are human, scientists and philosophers too disagree. And reason is not all on one side in the controversy. Perhaps the believers, too, may be moved "by profound reverence for the rationality made manifest in existence."

The late William James, in his *Varieties of Religious Experience*, in the chapter "The Positive Content of Religious Experience," declares:

Science . . . has ended by utterly repudiating the personal point of view. . . . The God whom science recognizes must be a God of universal laws exclusively, a God who does a wholesale, not a retail business. He cannot accommodate his processes to the convenience of individuals. . . . You see how natural it is, from this point of view, to treat religion as a mere survival. . . .

Then Professor James continues:

In spite of the appeal which this impersonality of the scientific attitude makes to a certain magnanimity of temper, I believe it to be shallow, and I can now state my reason in a comparatively few words. That reason is that, so long as we deal with the cosmic and the general, we deal only with the symbols of reality, *but as soon as we deal with private and personal phenomena as such, we deal with realities in the complete essence of the term.* . . . To describe the world with all the various feelings of the individual pinch of Destiny, all the various spiritual attitudes left out from the description—they being as describable as anything else—would be something like offering a printed bill of fare as the equivalent for a solid meal. Religion makes no such blunder. . . . It does not follow, because our ancestors made so many errors of fact and mixed them with their religion, that we should therefore leave off being religious at all. By being religious we establish ourselves in possession of ultimate reality at the only points at which reality is given us to guard.

I take it that what Professor James is really saying is that the thoughts that stir us, the hopes that lift us, the things of which we dream, our anxieties, our fears, our sacrifices in the name of right, beauty, friendship, and love are real, just as real as speed of light or the law of gravitation. The glory of a sunset may not be completely described in terms of the physicist, nor does the geological explanation of Grand Canyon tell the whole of its majesty.

A number of years ago, the late Dr. Frankwood E. Williams, distinguished psychiatrist and social analyst, published a paper (in the *Survey Graphic*, June, 1932) entitled "Out From Confusion," in which he declared that man was trapped by the dilemmas which he himself creates. He said, "God can't help. Religion is bankrupt; its leaders, pathetic failures." He proposed that man recognize the Devil in himself and adjust his ideals and principles accordingly. He appealed to man to yield to the "force within," which must be roused to action in behalf of the good, the true, and the beautiful.

I should like to ask, what is the source of this good, this true, and this beautiful to which these men appeal in the end? They who discount personal religion usually fall back upon some inner plus or power; and, indeed, this plus or power is the force which explains the prophetic insight of the social scientist and the cosmic mathematician. What is it? It is the spirit of man, it is man's instinctive acknowledgment of what is right, his capacity for friendship, the consciousness of brotherhood. These profound instincts in the spirit of man have been built up laboriously through the centuries, through the discipline of experience and ministrations of religion which always held up to man a picture of what he might be if he would.

Behind the formal side of religion, which is merely an effort to express the idea, there is the instinctive impulse of man to relate himself to the universe. Man came to feel that life is worth while, goodness is real, sacrifice is necessary, all things have meaning, *because he related himself to the eternal spirit.* It was just this conscious relation to God that validated all human experience. That was the dynamic that moved man.

When I say God I do not mean an old man with a flowing beard riding on a cloud; I do not mean an exalted Setebos of more human Calibans. I mean that mind and might, that will and love, that beauty and glory we sense in the world round about us and to which in our best moments we feel related in an intimate and personal way.

I try to do the decent, generous, social thing because when I do some change takes place within me. I feel enlargement and exaltation. But I want to do it most of all because my horizons are widened, because I am conscious then of a friendliness in the universe, of an intimacy with seas and stars as well as with my fellow men; because my life somehow seems caught up in the larger process of which I feel myself a worthy and necessary part; because my spirit for the moment seems to share in the cosmic process; because, in short, I then joyously recognize my kinship with God and my responsibility to myself and my fellow men.

Of course, I admit these things are not matters of scientific proof. There is no proof of God save that which rises out of the inmost being of a man. I know that not to all is given that poignant sense of His presence. I know too that religious institutions that have spoken in His name have all too often crucified His spirit.

It is out of such convictions, however, of which the institutions of religion are custodians, that the great social dynamic is born in the masses of men. Without these beliefs and the institutions created to give them expression, the social evolution becomes the social revolution. Without these civilizing, restraining, and socializing truths of religion, we build on sand, for there is nothing to underwrite the values to which man yields loyalty save a dark stoicism. With them we can build enduringly. Man becomes integrated in his universe. He will not feel that he struggles alone. He will not close his eyes to the evil in himself, but he will seek to subdue it; he will not ignore it, he will sublimate it because he believes in *a power within and without himself* that makes for righteousness.

There will always be those to whom the idea of a personal God means nothing. There will also always be those to whom it is the foundation, the source and inspiration for life. So far as religion is concerned, if it forswears the idea of a God-personality, of whom the human personality is but a vague reflection, it will have poured out of the vessel the wine of life. Amid all the differences of creed and dogma and theology, underpinning them all and the source from which they all derive, is the idea of the living God.

May I indicate, in conclusion, the task of the church and synagogue as I see it. Behind all the things that divide Jew and Christian, behind the differences in formal worship, our sectarian emphases and our sacraments and our ceremonies, we must pool the faith that is in us that justice is real and loving kindness more than a phrase, because God is!

Here is our world with its hungry to be fed, its naked to be clothed, its maimed and sick to be given shelter. Here is the world with its corruption in politics and the social order, with its religious prejudices, with its international hatreds. Here is a world at war! What a challenge to the religious forces of the nation! Men say: Where is God in all this holocaust of humanity? Beyond all differences in creed and ceremony, Christians and Jews must lift their voice and proclaim: God IS . . . the Eternal ruleth and in the end will conquer the world for truth and holiness and beauty, with the help of them who believe in Him, who believe where they cannot see, who trust where they cannot understand.

Christians and Jews, before the challenge of this common task to revive the faith of the world and the hearts of men within it, to work with God to build His Kingdom, let us be patient with each other, trusting each other, helping each other, working together for human liberty and justice and ordered progress in the name of the one Eternal God.

The Economic Factor in Religious Prejudice

By

HENRY NOBLE MacCRACKEN, Ph.D., LL.D., L.H.D.*

THE fundamental thing in democracy is the thesis of the Declaration of Independence: the right, not of life, liberty, and the pursuit of happiness, but of the people to change their rulers. This right is expressed in the Declaration as not revolution, but as ordered law. The American Revolution was not a revolution in any real sense, but a rebellion. Its essential procedure was that of legislatures adopting laws setting up an authority independent of a king. The fact that a regularly prosecuted war ensued should not blind us to the basic truth that the process was a legal one, and that the Americans throughout the war maintained a congress, duly chosen, and accepted by people of the several states.

The provisions of the constitution are democratic, because they provide for a periodical test of the wish of the people to change their rulers. Its design of checks and balances between executive and legislative, legislative and judicial, judicial and executive, is primarily the preservation of this right. Similarly the respective powers of the federal and state authorities are reserved in order that the people of the states may retain the same right. This function is the crucial test of democracy; everything else derives from it.

We who believe in the right of people to change their rulers by due process of law must always keep in mind that every legal process rests, in the last analysis, on public opinion. On us rests forever the obligation to teach democracy, so that the legal process which is organic may forever receive the life-giving sap of democracy from its roots in the hearts of the people. I conceive this meeting to be directed to this end.

We are met to consider what are the basic conditions in the soil of democracy from which the life-giving sap can be drawn for the nourishment of the organic process of democracy. What,

* President, Vassar College.

in other words, is essential in American life, in order that the people may take advantage of the process, and exercise of their rights to change their rulers without endangering the process?

Before we try to answer this question, we must first make clear why this elementary question need be asked at all. Is it not the very commonplace of the American way of life? Yes, it is a commonplace, but we need to state commonplaces over and over again, that each generation may understand what moves us, and so understanding, may approve our plan; and so approving, may give their minds to its support.

It is especially necessary in 1940, because this way of life is challenged by other ways, which are born of destitution and despair. Driven by economic conditions below the level of logical consideration, many peoples have been compelled to substitute economic survival for political thought. They have identified government with livelihood, and in order to survive have surrendered the right to change their rulers. They have placed their hope in an unchangeable party which has guaranteed them the conditions of existence, by asking them to give up all the higher values of spiritual, intellectual, and social intercourse which we know under the general term, civilization. The theory which has produced the world-wide disintegration of political thought, we know as economic determinism. Looking out upon the great changes of industrial society, men have mistaken these mechanisms for ideas, and have affirmed that there are no longer ideas, but only things. The logic based upon these things they call by different names, national socialism and communism being the most widespread. Whatever their name, they agree in one great principle, that the industrial process is the one great fact, or cause, and that all political theory derives from it. They have mistaken the result for the cause. Industrial development came as the result of political freedom, which gave peace to the world, protection to invention, and world-wide markets for industrial products. In the name of industrialism they have destroyed these results. They have created war, they have enslaved the inventive mind, and they have annihilated the free commerce among peoples. Thus the process is reversed and the peoples who put their faith in the industrial process as the sole condition of life have made it impossible for industrialism to survive. In no country where political freedom is gone, has industrialism prospered. But by the use, or rather by the misuse, of the benefits derived from a long period of political government, they have invented a nationalism which is really a reversion to the older theories of government, a despotism with accompanying enslavement of subject peoples.

How did this come about? It came about because of the failure of those nations which had adopted the political theory of democracy to extend the principles of democracy to the rest of the world. We kept democracy for ourselves, but did not wish others to have it. There was no legal process, no world constitution, by which we could extend it. This it was for which Woodrow Wilson struggled, and which in the League of Nations he tried to make explicit. The war of 1939 is the logical outcome of the failure of his ideas to win the adhesion of the people.

Of a certain ruler of the Hebrews, Jeshurun, it is written that he waxed fat, and kicked. The abounding prosperity of the Americans led them first to forget the source of prosperity, namely, the political conditions that had made them possible, and then to erect as their idol the very prosperity that had been given them under free institutions.

Bitter necessity is now upon us of retracing our steps. Unemployment and the collapse of our financial system have forced upon us a reconsideration of the nature of democracy, and of the conditions which nourish it. The revalues of the great imperialisms, our own among them, have produced conditions which compel us to go back to political thinking, in order that we may clear our minds of the great economic fallacy, and set our feet again on the American way of life.

The great economic fallacy is this, that man lives by bread alone. The great Teacher of the Christian religion told us that man did not live by bread alone, but by every word that proceeded out of the mouth of God, by ideas, in other words, which derived their truth from the divine source of truth. Christ did not deny that economics existed, or that it was unimportant. He taught only that we must put the Kingdom of God first, and all the economic sufficiency would then be added unto us. This, in a word, is the true way to which we must return. The great Hebrew prophets taught the same lesson. In them we find the same categorical demand, that we first define our values, then live by them, and that as a result peace and

plenty will return. The world has laughed at this simple teaching, and bitterly has it paid for its scorn.

We who meet here today, under the auspices of a great university of free learning, agree, I think, about these things. We
are here to defend American liberties, which are the product
of our political thought. We are not here to defend religion.
Totalitarianism destroys religious institutions. It can never
destroy religion. Itself survives only by borrowing the code of
religious institutions. The truth of religion survives. Our aim
is, by making clear the religious basis of life on which political
thought is built, to restore faith in that political thought, and
so to maintain the divine right of the human soul to freedom.

It is, therefore, obligatory upon us to point out that the great
economic fallacy, that man lives by bread alone, is a virus that
has poisoned many wells that gave the water of life to mankind.
If I confine myself to one such well today, it is only as an
illustration of the general truth. If I discuss the economic causes
of religious intolerance, it is not because I think them to be a
separate stream of causation. It is not because they are inevitable,
given the conditions. The economic aspects of religious and
other prejudice are simply the result of our failure to live by
the truth of our religion and the political system we have
evolved from it.

Religious prejudices, in short, are simply economic prejudices
manifesting themselves among groups of professedly religious
persons. They are inseparable from an economic process that
has been allowed to develop independently of the law and the
gospel. Innumerable other prejudices have accompanied religious intolerance. Regional prejudice is one; it existed before
our constitution as a nation. North against South, large province
against small province, slaveholder against free agriculture,
fishing against tobacco, these are but a few of the economic
causes of rivalry and resulting prejudice. Immigration had already set in, and here in Quaker Philadelphia there was a bitter
prejudice against the Scots and Scots Irish settlements; and
these in turn bitterly resented their taxation by a government
that gave them little support against the Indians. Prejudices
resulted from the inability of the European to comprehend the
continental interests of our people. Rivers made prejudice, and
mountains, and lakes. Some districts were open for trade and
growth, others were isolated and became static. Slow-moving

communities resented the spread of tolerance in commercial centers. A few years ago, when under the auspices of the Calvert Associates, I pleaded by radio that religious intolerance should not prevent impartial consideration of Al Smith's candidacy. I was amazed by the torrent of intolerance that was mailed to me from Pennsylvania and the Alleghenies. The letters were analyzed, and were found to be most numerous from the Allegheny Mountains. The same mountains that were the refuge of liberty in dark days had become an abode of intolerance.

Racial prejudice in America long preceded the advent of Jews in large numbers. With each successive wave of alien culture—Scottish, Irish, German, Italian, Hungarian, Polish, Russian—arose a corresponding wave of prejudice against the poor immigrants, who caused temporary fluctuations in the labor market, and whose value as potential consumers was ignored. The cultural lag of these groups, especially where language was a problem, further enhanced the prejudice, which rationalizing carried further. When religion was added, it was but one more factor in this grand process of rationalization, by which economic jealousy acted behind a smoke screen of patriotic puritanism. So long as there were free lands, and the waves of migrants passed to the west, there was not so much antagonism; but when the Irish settled in New York and Boston, and became the dominant political group, religious differences were added to the economic jealousies. Until lately, however, our political institution stood the strain. Only with the Negro did they fail, and even here religious work among the slaves alleviated some of the prejudice.

It took a major economic crisis to convert religious prejudice into a great political issue. There were Know-Nothings and American Parties, and A.P.A. in former times, but these were ephemeral. The deeper religious intolerances did not come to the surface until our time.

New students at Vassar, a residential college, are distributed throughout the houses. Jews are not encouraged to live together. No sororities or other exclusive clubs are allowed. Catholics and Protestants room together. If our national economy had been run on similar lines, there would have been less prejudice. But Jews gathered in great ghettos. Poles went into heavy industry, Negroes multiplied in the deep South. Self-preservation became the rule of life for the older dominant groups, and real assimilation was retarded. Of the Polish Catholics, I know more from first-hand experience than of other groups, as I have been president of the Kosciuszko Foundation for intellectual relations with Poland for the past fifteen years. I know there are only two kinds of Poles in America; the 100% Americans and the 200% Americans. Their reaction from life in German or Russian Poland was so great that they embraced democracy with fervor. They were a democracy-loving people before they came; and in the new soil their democracy grew luxuriantly. But everywhere they were confronted with the strong intolerance of the older Protestant group, and in this chill atmosphere they naturally stuck together, and became politically self-conscious.

Change, growth, mobility, adaptation, adjustment; these are the essential ingredients of democracy. Wherever they are stopped, democracy itself is threatened. By endeavoring to prevent a change of rule, the older groups, numerically inferior, were really undermining the democratic process, and they have paid bitterly for it. Racial concentration in American industrial centers, caused by this prejudice, are today the centers where alien ideologies flourish. Democracy is there only imperfectly understood.

So we came gradually to see that we could not allow economic processes to work independently in such places. We came to see that democracy must permeate the whole industrial structure if it was to be preserved. We have, I think, weathered the worst of the gale, but there is much to be done before we make the harbor.

Many of the immigrant groups came to us as religious communities. This was true of the Pennsylvania Germans. It is equally true of Italians. In Poughkeepsie a whole Sicilian parish transferred itself to the bank of the Hudson. For a long time it lived by itself, to itself. But in late years this isolation has faded, and today the Italian group is on good terms with the rest, Americans all, immigrants all.

In my opinion, all we need to make democracy work is to make religion work. God gave us, by his laws of the universe, evolution and the rest, certain powers and capacities which he desired us to use. We can use them only in freedom. Democracy is man's device to put them to work, a system which alone permits of free movement from place to place and from station to station in life. If we put God first, and our fancied economic interest second, we shall find that in this way alone is the highest economic advantage obtained; for the highest economic interest is identical with the highest religious principle and the highest political plan. It is this: the highest employment of the best capacity God has given us. Let us not confuse ourselves with words. There is one God, and one mankind, the one deriving from the other.

A corollary of the democratic dogma of the right of people to change their rulers by constitutional process is the right of people to diversity, in thought, in religion, in social ways. Diversity of creatures, to use Kipling's phrase, is also a condition of economic progress. Unity in diversity, expressed in our motto, E Pluribus Unum, is a spiritual one, not forced, but the result of logical thought, and of democratic life. The totalitarian state, which affirms economic uniformity, really crushes out all true economic progress. We Americans should study our economic history, to discover how economic progress came from the wide diversity of occupation, the increasing diversity of physical needs, and satisfactions. We are, for example, a nation that literally lives on wheels. Nowhere else in the world is there such travel, such interest in diversity of contact and experience. If life were uniform, there would be no incentive to travel, no automobiles. The uniformity of living which was expected to result from mass production has not occurred. Instead, an immense variety of experience, through our highways, our national and state forests and reservations, has come about. These in turn have promoted an immense variety of human contacts.

Not long ago, a Chinese woman at Vassar got off a bus. The driver said to me, "Doc, I was fifteen years in China, in the U. S. Marines, and I seen a lot of them Chinamen, and let me tell you something; they're human, the same as us." He enunciated a great truth. By diversity of contact, due to economic freedom, we make for understanding.

No one denies that democracy is the most difficult of all governments to maintain. It requires intelligence and education to participate in democracy. A wide variation in educational opportunity and advancement tends to weaken democracy. So, too, in an economic system, variations in skill may make for prejudice. In New England, Yankees no longer able to make a living from sparse Connecticut soil have been driven out by Slovaks accustomed to intensive farming. The prejudice excited by a sense of inferiority as farmers is attached to the religion of the newcomers.

This inferiority is not restricted to purely economic processes. A few days ago, I was a guest at a dinner of music-lovers. My tablemate burst into a tirade against the Jews for monopolizing music in America. A few minutes' talk brought out the real cause of the complaint; it was inferiority as a musician. Of the musical background of the Jew, of the centuries of training, of the realization that with similar opportunity and advantages, success in music might come to the Gentile, there was no comprehension. It is inevitable that in a new country just awakening to a knowledge of art, music, and the theatre, the well-trained European will rise to the top.

Prevented by European custom from land cultivation, the Jew turned long ago to the arts. A great premium was placed on education, his only path to equality. Medicine had been his gift to Europe. It was natural that he should turn to it. But the prejudice against Jewish physicians is so great that a quota system has been raised against it, which now operates even in state institutions. In the younger branches, such as psychiatry, the Jews have had greater freedom, and are now so numerous that anti-semitism has attached itself to this whole branch of medicine.

This leads me to the observation that a long-maintained practice of prejudice gradually affects the mental attitude of its victims. Thus the economic rivalry actually injures men as workers and producers. When shall we learn the lesson that men are men, not units in a machine? that moral factors are far more influential than those that come from physical environment?

One source of prejudice from economic causes, which affects all religious groups, is the impression in labor circles that the church is indifferent to their rights. This is especially strong in localities where labor is from younger racial groups, whose social relations are not with the older and more settled churches. In recent years this feeling has been very strong. It has led to the social organization of churches. The Protestant Federal Council of Churches has labored mightily with the leaders of industry for shorter hours and better working conditions. The Catholics have originated unique experiments in coöperative living such as that in Nova Scotia, and in the Chicago stockyard district. Jewish religious leaders have been among the foremost in improving conditions in the great textile industry. It can no longer be said that the church as a whole is indifferent, although social inertia still is prejudicial in many communities.

The fact is clear that the church, as distinct from religion, has been almost as much affected by the great economic fallacy as other human institutions. If it is in any degree less so, it is because a spark of true religion is still to be found among the solid pewholders of this generation. The church has tried to salve its conscience with philanthropy, and its record is indeed most creditable. Our country is most generous. But our Master knew well that unless the heart is changed, and we have true charity, it availeth nothing.

I have served in community chests where ministers of different churches in the same town worked together for the first time, burying religious prejudice in the interest of the common welfare. Here the church followed, where it should have led. Nothing has done more for mutual good will in our cities than common work for the Red Cross. But it does not go far enough. Each group is left in its own work of participation. Only the leaders share in mutual understanding. New pressures seem to be needed to break up the social divisions that now characterize American life. Can these come from the church, or must we wait till a new war makes us all Americans?

What I have been trying to say amounts only to this, that while economic processes have undoubtedly created situations in which religious intolerance has arisen, the blame cannot rest on economics. The real sin is a spiritual one, when we accept economic situations as inevitable. If we once accept the thesis that man lives by bread alone, we become a willing prey to all baser motives.

Only by realizing that man is a whole being, that his spiritual nature is his ultimate and determining one, shall we ever solve these problems. Man must be free to worship; he must also be free to change himself. He can do this only if he takes charge of his own destiny. To do this he must be free from the consequences of his own passions. He must live in law and in order.

He must be free to change his rulers in an orderly way, whenever new rulers are needed. The most orderly way is the most stable way. The spiritual faith in man's divine rights as a free soul leads inevitably, in my opinion, to some form of free government. I know of no better one at this time than democracy. But to make democracy work the true religion must permeate it at every point, most of all in the economic process. Instead of economics entering the church to dictate its life and action, the current must be reversed. Religion must enter economics, until men ask, Is this right? before they ask, Is this profitable?

All this requires patience, patience, and again patience, especially of those who do not think as we do.

It is significant that this symposium is held under the auspices of a great university which traces its origin from an academy advocated by Benjamin Franklin two hundred years ago. Franklin was an apostle of toleration in an age when even the good Quakers of Philadelphia, corrupted by wealth and position, were not free from the vice of ill will. For them he wrote a fable, which he called the "Fifty-first chapter of Genesis." He printed it as a Bible leaf, and used to read it to his visitors in this City of Brotherly Love. As it is less known than it should be, I take the liberty of quoting it in full, in tribute to a great Founder of a great university:

Genesis 51

1 And it came to pass after these things that Abraham sat in the door of his tent, about the going down of the sun.

2 And behold a man bent with age coming from the way of the wilderness, leaning upon a staff.

3 And Abraham arose and met him and said unto him, Turn in, I pray thee and wash thy feet, and tarry all night, and thou shalt arise early in the morning, and go on thy way.

4 And the man said, Nay for I will abide under this tree.

5 But Abraham pressed him greatly as he turned and they went into the tent; and Abraham baked unleavened bread and they did eat.

6 And when Abraham saw that the man blessed not God, he said unto him, Wherefore dost thou not worship the most high God, creator of heaven and earth?

7 And the man answered and said I do not worship thy God neither do I call upon his name; for I have made to myself a god

which abideth always in mine house, and provideth me with all things.

8 And Abraham's zeal was kindled against the man and he arose and fell upon him and drove him forth with blows into the wilderness.

9 And God called unto Abraham saying, Abraham where is the stranger?

10 And Abraham answered and said, Lord, he would not worship thee neither would he call upon thy name; therefore have I driven him forth from before my face into the wilderness.

11 And God said, Have I borne with him these hundred and ninety and eight years and nourished him and cloathed him, notwithstanding his rebellion against me; and couldst not thou, who art thyself a sinner, bear with him one night?

The Political Aspect of
Christian-Jewish Relations

By

GEORGE NAUMAN SHUSTER, Ph.D.*

IT WAS an eighteenth-century tract writer who said of freedom that only God could have thought of it and that only man can forget. And, quite obviously, all the great crises in history are concerned with freedom, because every such crisis is of and in that spirit of man the essence of which is freedom. Does the statement need proof? One might appeal to the theologians and the philosophers, the historians and the political scientists. But in these days it may be easier and equally wise to appeal to the experience of the average man, adrift in the darkness that has engulfed the earth. Today there are whole nations which can only with difficulty remember that they were once free, and with still greater difficulty fancy that they may some-time be free again. And more appalling still is the fact that this erasure of liberty is most complete in those lands in which Christianity, despite almost unceasing heterodoxy, had made sacred the cult of the free person. So far has this negation of seemingly established values progressed that countless millions of our fellow men, who only a few years ago lived otherwise, now doubt whether they have any right to think that truth differs from falsehood, brutality from humaneness, labor from servitude. For them the most routine ethical statements no longer have any validity. You may say, "So-and-So is an honest man." They will answer, "Does he belong to the Party?" You may go on to add, "He has spent his life doing good to others"; and the response will be, "But what has he done for the Leader?"

Only after one has tried to survey and to understand this disturbing upheaval can one fruitfully approach the problem of the relations between Christian and Jew as a political fact. That problem is, of course, other things, too, than a political

* President, Hunter College.

fact. So much has been made clear by my colleagues. Unless substantiated by what they have said, my remarks will have little value. A polity cannot be studied unless one bears in mind the economic enterprise in which citizens more or less collectively engage, or the moral and religious values by which the outlook of the individual is governed. But the polity is law and its enforcement. It is, on the one hand, reason creating recognition for rights, and on the other hand that awesome and dangerous resolution to enforce recognition which we call police power. The difference between civilization and its opposite lies first of all in the following query and its answer: To what extent does law enshrine reason and rights, and to what extent does the police power exact respect for that reason and those rights?

This is why the status of the Jew has become for practically every thoughtful Christian the decisive element in our contemporary situation. One may not know any Jews. One may dislike those one knows. The Hebraic ritual may be distasteful; the business efficiency of Jewish merchants may arouse feelings of jealousy and anger. Still all these things and more cannot legitimately render one indifferent to the manner in which the polity by which one's own civilization is determined deals with the Jew. The Christian in particular cannot be indifferent. For quite apart from the fact that he must respect the inalienable rights of every fellow being, he necessarily looks upon the Jew as a believer in a great religion allied as no other can be with his own. You may retort at this point that historical Christianity has itself persecuted the Jew, and the statement is certainly worth considering briefly. The law of the medieval Christian polity was clear and firm in its denunciation of the pogroms. Pope and Council, saint and doctor, agreed in their hostility to violence and oppression. What was at fault was enforcement of the law—what failed was the police power. Medieval civilization was one long struggle for the control of that power, and we are fully aware of the weaknesses and the corruption which resulted from that struggle. But the law itself, though imperfect, was good; and every Christian of our time cannot do otherwise than wish it had been lived up to then and that it may be lived up to now. Moreover, even at their worst the popular excesses of the medieval period did not commit the ghastly crime of annihilating the Jew as a person. They were products of moods current in a period of religious wars. If the Jew abandoned his faith, he was molested no longer. The question was what he believed, not what he was.

I can well imagine that the Jew, like the member of any other minority, may suffer comparable though lesser disadvantages even in a free society. He may be compelled to hide his keeping of the Sabbath Day or his addiction to kosher food if he would avoid the peril of seeming to be different from his fellows. It may be suggested to him that he cease spending money on the development of Palestine, or stop belonging to Jewish organizations exclusively. And if he obeys out of deference to the surrounding majority, he may find in the end that he has wasted his spiritual substance and is despised for his weakness. Yet though that sort of pressure might conceivably be so irksome as to constitute real persecution, it would still be as different as day is from night from the terror of a polity which annulled his freedom and enforced the annulment.

This difference is of such central importance that our time will be judged by it. But strangely enough many of us fail to understand it. We confuse the fatal, cancerous disease which is now destroying the life of Europe with the merely malodorous pestilence of anti-Semitism. I have often tried to make the point clear with an illustration. Suppose that a Jew were really guilty of all the crimes which demagogues attribute to his race. Let us imagine that he had been brought to book for conducting a fraudulent international bank; for spreading subversive doctrines and undermining morals; for ritual murder and the willful corruption of youth. Grant that the evidence was incontrovertible. In a society which fosters the traditions of Western Europe, he would nevertheless be brought to trial, convicted, and sentenced as an individual. He would be treated as is every other free man who is guilty of crime. He would be innocent until proved guilty.

When, however, a society has ceased to have any relationship with the norms of Western civilization, things like these happen. The Nazis arrived in Vienna, and the director of a Jewish foundling hospital, endowed and maintained with Jewish alms, was suddenly notified that the babies must be removed from the institution within forty-eight hours. With difficulty a vacant house was secured. One hour before the evacuation, an order was given that no property could be removed. The children were therefore carried naked through the streets. But I shall not go on; I have seen so much that has turned my stomach and frozen my heart that I cannot any longer bring myself to report the infamy—the shameless infamy—which every resident in Central Europe has seen reflected in countless unforgettable episodes during these dreadful years. What is staggering is not this or that pogrom, this or that brutal deed, but the perversion of law, the transformation of a concept of man into a concept of animal. Yes, there once was Negro slavery which some who are still alive can remember. But even the institution of slavery, which was a product of European man's imperfect insight into savage civilizations, had a code which by comparison with what is now set up in Europe was humane and enlightened. The facts reported from a thousand places, not by gossips or partisans but by the most unimpeachable witnesses— for example, the decent men in the German army itself—are so horrifying that if one did not strive to blot them from one's mind one should have no time to do anything else. One would simply be galvanized into an attitude of despair before forces which must sometime, somehow, be challenged and defeated.

Now one cannot make a polity inhuman in one respect without dehumanizing it in its entirety. That was evident in theory; it is now manifest also in practice. There have disappeared all the rights of minorities and all the rights of individuals. The issue is now not merely Solon *versus* Lycurgus—whether men shall be governed by Spartan martial law, or by legislation fostering life in a cultured community. Nor is the question properly one of the merits or demerits of parliamentary institutions, for a society without such institutions might well respect the basic non-political liberties of the person. What we confront as a growing threat to ourselves is a polity in which, for having spoken against the sex morality of Rosenberg or the biology of Hitler, Protestant and Catholic clergymen are sentenced to long terms in concentration camps under an emergency decree banning Communistic activity; in which property is not collectivized, with or without compensation, but is expropriated willfully and whimsically; in which children are made the traps with which their fathers are ensnared, and motherhood turned into an addendum to the science of ballistics.

These are some of the goals to which crafty exploitation of anti-Semitic feeling has led. Few of those Germans who, in the early thirties, applauded the slogans of Hitler and Goebbels had any idea that they were doomed to witness what has since come to pass; and it must be conceded that relatively few in the world outside understood either. For that world was not prepared for so signal and startling a repudiation of values, nor is prepared now to face the bleak truth that civilization as we have known it inside the boundaries of Europe may cease to exist for generations. To be sure, we know from history that long-range pessimism is the least tenable of philosophies. But one can scarce doubt either the night which has fallen upon Europe, or the dire portent of that darkness for the countries of the New World. Is it not merely that there seems to be a sequence of ideologies, both there and here. More fundamental is the fact that against maladies which beset the human spirit no distance is any longer a barrier.

Who then can doubt that there is a genuine need for an effort to prevent the easiest of the incipient stages of dictatorship—the attack on the rights of minorities, particularly the rights of the Jew? What form that effort might desirably take is a question no one can decide. I shall offer an opinion which is frankly only an opinion. Let us not begin by placing the emphasis on anti-Semitism. For anti-Semitism is, within limits, a quite natural and normal emotion in times when nationalistic frenzy makes group cohesion the very basis of culture. If Catholics are perennial targets by reason of their religion alone, then the Jew—who is separated from his fellow men by a creed, by an especial historical heritage, and by the fact that he belongs like the Armenian and the Syrian to the Near Eastern folk group—must expect to be even more persistently attacked by minority baiters. To talk incessantly of anti-Semitism, or anti-Catholicism, is to foment the very disease one is trying to combat. The emphasis should be placed, I think, upon the conservation of the polity. If we can educate the great majority of our fellow citizens into awareness of what human rights are and of the basic obligation of society to conserve those rights through law, we shall have reared a solid bulwark of conviction against the onslaught of totalitarian ideologies from abroad.

This education is, I believe, one of the great immediate mandates of the Christian social gospel. It seems to me that while the totalitarian revolt against the Western World is a complex phenomenon, its essential characteristic is this—that while nationalistic religions are being fanned into a fanaticism which renders the chauvinism of the nineteenth century tepid and genteel by comparison, there is in progress at the very same time a social conflict which cuts straight across national boundaries. This conflict is wider than the gap between Communists and capitalists. It includes that, to be sure, but it includes also the venomous disagreement between those once privileged either in property or position and the organized and politically moderate labor groups. Thus in Germany Hitler recruited well-wishers from amongst all those whom military defeat and social welfare legislation alike had impoverished. The Weimar Republic had been the formal expression of Social Democracy as conceived of by an organized labor fundamentally pacifistic, progressive, and committed to the alleviation of social distress. And in practice it was the member of a Trades Union and his family who benefited by the legislation which transformed Germany from an autocratic Prussian monarchical state into a very democratic and anti-militaristic state. Meanwhile, however, the abolition of the army and the navy, inflation, and heavy social taxes had greatly affected not only the privileged classes of yore but also that vast group of citizens with a little property and a little prestige, to whom the term "middle class" applies. Very many who detested the Nazi doctrine and subscribed in no wise to the polity it projected nevertheless supported Hitler because they wanted above all the defeat of privileged labor. The triumph of the Fuehrer was in all truth a revolution which led to a goal that the majority of its supporters had not visualized at all. Nor did the Nazi ability to reap the harvest of social antagonism stop with the conquest of the German people. In virtually all the smaller countries of postwar Europe, similar conflicts were impeding. The "Fifth Column" everywhere comprises those who would rather oppose hated social groups in their own country than make common cause with them against the national enemy, though paradoxically enough they are nevertheless rabid janissaries of the creed of nationalism. It is hard to believe that France's most violent chauvinists were prepared to give the Hitler salute. But it is true, even as the same thing is true of Austria, Czechoslovakia, Holland, and Belgium.

These phenomena are difficult to account for. Nevertheless it is clear that the violent moods, hatreds, and remorseless cruelty of the present are to a very great extent the fruits of a sense of moral outrage. People saw their fortunes swept away by an inflation which brought wealth to speculators and philanderers; they saw thousands sink into poverty, and those who had shirked their duty rise to affluence on a wave of pacifist feeling; and they came to believe that behind the pompous façade of international conference-making there was only the gambler, the merchant, and the intriguer. In short, men lost faith not merely in the integrity of the men who led them, but also in the polity to which they owed allegiance. They had lost the conviction that their rights were sacred or safe. Life even had been stripped of its sanction. The law of the jungle was, therefore, invoked anew.

That anti-Semitism should have played the rôle it has in the upheaval which followed Germany's recourse to vengeance is to a considerable extent accidental. Yet by no means wholly so. Hitler, of course, happened to come from Austria, pre-war hotbed of conflicting nationalist madnesses, where Judaism was tainted with antipathy to the German, and Pan-Germanism with a blind hatred of the Jew. Hitler himself was afflicted with the *Geltungsbeduerfnis* of the mestizo. But one must also note that, exception being made for resolute Catholic and Protestant minorities, Christians in the whole of Central Europe were far more concerned with partisanship than they were with the polity. They were so eager to safeguard positions within the state itself. I venture to think this was a betrayal of their most fundamental social principles. For what could be more contradictory in terms than belief in a universal religion based on the equal sacredness of all men, and failure to realize that a pogrom is a farewell to the idea that any human being is of sacred importance? Men said and thought that Christians should protect themselves and not jeopardize their own position through benevolence for the Jew. And in so doing they not only forgot one-half of the New Testament but they undermined their own security more completely than they could otherwise have done had they tried.

In this country rabid anti-Semitism of the kind described will not be an accident. It will be and is being preached by the large group of those who for one reason or another desire the world-wide triumph of the Fascist idea. If social antagonism grows stronger in our midst, if it should prove impossible to foster conciliation between labor and the middle class, these

Fascist apostles may succeed. But at least this is true: Christians are no longer under any illusions. The terrifying experiences through which they have lived have made the essential things plain. We shall not be able to conserve Christianity except as a scattered handful of imperiled believers unless we can preserve the polity which our fathers patterned, however faultily, after Christian ideals. I think that to a vast throng Christianity is still the deepest, the most beautiful, the most abiding of the forces which make up the life of mankind. I believe this throng will stand firm. It will have faith in God and man sufficient unto victory.